PRAISE FOR *JOURNEY TO LASTING HAPPINESS*

Linda's *Journey to Lasting Happiness* is an exceptional guide, echoing her electrifying presence at our summit where she captivated all. Her book, a meticulously crafted road map, intertwines storytelling and wisdom, empowering readers with tools for transformative self-discovery. Through workbook exercises, interactive videos, and reflective sessions, Linda's work isn't just a book; it's a beacon of hope guiding readers toward enduring happiness and boundless joy. With Linda as their guide, readers embark on a journey of profound growth and radiant vitality.

—NICK NANTON, ESQ.
CEO/FOUNDING PARTNER, ASTONISH ENTERTAINMENT; EMMY
AWARD–WINNING DIRECTOR AND PRODUCER; BEST-SELLING AUTHOR

You can transform your biggest problems into your biggest blessings by reading Linda Allred's book *Journey to Lasting Happiness*. Her amazing and fun self-healing techniques guide you to harness your unlimited ability to successfully heal yourself!

—PAMELA WINKLER, PhD
PRESIDENT, ST. JOHN'S UNIVERSITY

Linda's book is an absolute gem! With her engaging storytelling and authentic Southern charm, Linda captivates readers and empowers them to unlock their true potential!

—NANCY MATTHEWS
SPEAKER; AUTHOR; FOUNDER, THE PEOPLE SKILLS ACADEMY

If you want your life to be transformed, then Linda's *Journey to Lasting Happiness* is the book for you. She offers a beacon of hope and inspiration, a comprehensive tool kit for personal growth and empowerment.

—TRISH CARR
AWARD-WINNING SPEAKER, CONSULTANT, COACH

Linda's *Journey to Lasting Happiness* offers a proven system for personal transformation. This book is a must-read for anyone seeking lasting positive change.

—LISA SASEVICH, "THE QUEEN OF SALES CONVERSION"

If you're ready to go from just seeking fulfillment to actually having the fulfillment in life you deserve, I encourage you to let Linda be your trusted guide on the path to lasting happiness, radiant health, and profound success.

—RAVEN BLAIR GLOVER, AKA "THE TALK SHOW MAVEN"

Linda's *Journey to Lasting Happiness* is a powerful tool for personal growth and transformation. With her comprehensive system, readers are equipped with practical strategies for achieving lasting happiness and success. Through engaging storytelling and profound insights, Linda empowers individuals to embrace change and live authentically. This book is a must-read for anyone seeking to unlock their inner potential and embark on a journey of self-discovery.

—LORAL LANGEMEIER
AUTHOR, *THE MILLIONAIRE MAKER*

JOURNEY TO

LASTING

HAPPINESS

Published by Impact Publishing®, Lake Mary, FL.
Impact Publishing® is a registered trademark.

ISBN: 979-8-9892734-7-8
LCCN: 2024914065

This publication is designed to provide accurate and authoritative information with regard to the subject matter covered. It is sold with the understanding that the publisher is not engaged in rendering legal, accounting, or other professional advice. If legal advice or other expert assistance is required, the services of a competent professional should be sought. The opinions expressed by the author in this book are not endorsed by Impact Publishing® and are the sole responsibility of the author rendering the opinion.

Most Impact Publishing® titles are available at special quantity discounts for bulk purchases for sales promotions, premiums, fundraising, and educational use. Special versions or book excerpts can also be created to fit specific needs.

For more information, please write:

Impact Publishing®
P.O. Box 950370
Lake Mary, FL 32746
Tel: 1.877.261.4930

Legal Notice: This system contains information gathered from many sources as well as from the experiences of the author and a number of her clients. It is published for general reference and not as a substitute for independent verification by users when circumstances warrant. It is sold with the understanding that neither the author nor the publisher is engaged in rendering any legal, accounting, or psychological advice. In instances where the opinions or advice of a legal, financial, psychological, or other professional is appropriate, such professional counsel should be sought. The publisher and author disclaim any liability whatsoever for individual use of any advice or information presented within the system. Although the author and publisher have used care and diligence in the preparation of this system, we assume no responsibility for errors or omissions.

Scripture quotations marked NKJV are taken from the New King James Version®. Copyright © 1982 by Thomas Nelson. Used by permission. All rights reserved.

Printed in the United States of America

JOURNEY TO

LASTING

HAPPINESS

A GUIDE TO LIVING A HAPPY, HEALTHY, AND SUCCESSFUL LIFE

LINDA ALLRED

Lake Mary, FL

I DEDICATE THIS BOOK TO MY HIGHER POWER, GOD, WHO WHISPERED, "LINDA, IT IS TIME TO WRITE YOUR BOOK NOW—THERE ARE MORE PEOPLE YOU NEED TO HELP," AS WELL AS TO ALL WOMEN WHO HAVE EVER FELT AS IF THEY WERE NOT GOOD ENOUGH!

CONTENTS

FOREWORD

M Y NAME IS Nikkea B. Devida. You may not know me yet, but I'm here to tell you about a journey—one that involves overcoming some of life's toughest challenges through healing from the inside out.

My own path of healing has been anything but straightforward, marked by my time in the Air Force, battles with post-traumatic stress disorder (PTSD), military sexual trauma (MST), anxiety, and an eating disorder, bulimia. Yet it's also been a journey of discovery, particularly in understanding the power of healing through sound science and the subconscious mind.

I first met Linda Allred back in 2009, when we both joined Lisa Sasevich's Sales Authenticity & Success Mastermind. It wasn't long after that Linda became one of the first to dive into the Accelerated Change Template (ACT)™ Virtual Bootcamp I offered, revised and relaunched under the new name, MindSonix, making the leap from my live workshops to this new online format. With Linda's background in hypnosis, she picked up MindSonix with incredible speed, and she quickly became one of my first hand-selected and trusted Certified MindSonix Practitioners.

Since then, Linda has been nothing short of a guiding light for hundreds, including me. Through her mastery of MindSonix she's helped people enhance every aspect of their lives—from health and relationships to careers and finances. I've had the privilege of co-facilitating workshops with her, witnessing her remarkable ability to transform lives firsthand. The Wheel of Life exercise in this book is a testament to Linda's expertise, providing you with a powerful tool to assess and improve various areas of your life swiftly and effectively.

But why is Linda uniquely qualified to guide you through this book? With over three decades of dedication to understanding the mind and using tools such as hypnosis and MindSonix to foster healing, Linda's expertise is unmatched. Beyond her professional credentials, Linda's personal journey of overcoming profound tragedies with grace and resilience is truly inspiring. Her strength, courage, and unwavering positive outlook on life are a beacon for anyone seeking to move from struggle to self-mastery.

As you embark on the journey this book offers, I encourage you to engage deeply with the exercises Linda presents. Whether you're already aware of areas in your life you'd like to improve or you're simply curious, there's something in these pages for you. Even if you feel your life is going well, Linda's insights can help you achieve your aspirational goals more swiftly and with greater clarity.

So take a moment to sit back, relax, and open yourself to the transformation that awaits. Linda's wisdom, coupled with your willingness to explore and change, can lead to profound shifts in your life. Here's to your journey to wholeness, and to Linda, for being an incredible guide along the way.

With warmth and anticipation for your transformation.

—NIKKEA B. DEVIDA
MINDSONIX INC. FOUNDER AND CEO

INTRODUCTION

I T STILL AMAZES me that some people go their whole lives never understanding the power of their own voice.

But when you grow up thinking you're inadequate, you run the risk of never truly understanding the power that your voice holds.

I didn't grow up in poverty, and I wasn't physically abused. But I did grow up with an alcoholic father who ignored me. Then at seventeen I married a man who was the complete opposite of my father. He talked to me all the time and told me what he liked about me (and sometimes what he didn't like). During the hard years of our marriage I never felt I could do anything right for my husband, Don. He'd find a flaw in everything I tried. Eventually, I started to hate myself, had no self-confidence, and was eating my pain away.

Sadly, at age forty-six, that was the story of my life. I started to feel pains in my chest and thought they were symptoms of a heart attack. The doctor told me my heart was fine, but he thought the pain was caused by stress. He told me to go learn how to relax.

During this time, I was plagued with negative thoughts about myself, such as, "I'm inadequate," or, "I'm not good enough." Once a person steps onto that crazy train, those thoughts gather incredible speed, an no emergency brake on earth can stop them. One of the issues between us was that Don had a college degree and I didn't. I always felt as though I'd receive his approval if I could just earn a degree.

One day I decided enough was enough—I would go get that degree. During the day, I worked in the Human Resources Department, and at night I started taking college classes at LSU. In one of my courses on business education, 75 percent of our final grade involved giving a presentation on a company of our choice. I found myself standing wide-eyed in front of a group of twenty-year-old college students in a state of absolute terror and panic.

Now, I don't know if you've ever experienced a panic attack from stage fright, but I can tell you it is not pretty. My voice was trembling. I was nauseated. Palms sweating. Thoughts scattered.

"My n-name is L-Linda. The name of my c-company is—" As I looked at the audience, their eyeballs got bigger and bigger the longer I spoke. I remember praying to God, "Please, just let me die."

When it was all over, the instructor asked me to stay after class. I told her, "You don't have to tell me. I know I made an F." She handed me an A for having the courage to complete the presentation. I was shocked.

Once I got home, I ran into the den, sat in my husband's lap, and sobbed. But I took that experience and said to myself, "OK, I have a problem. I need to learn to do better."

I attended speech communication classes while at LSU; then I enrolled in Toastmasters, a global organization that helps people build their communication and leadership skills. (Back then, you had to pay a penny every time you said, "Um." Last I heard, it was a nickel, but it's been years.) I then joined the National Speakers Association in New Orleans.

I was doing anything and everything I could to improve my speaking skills. But despite all the practice, I held on to a limiting belief that was keeping me from realizing my potential. I'll tell you more about that later in the book, but for now I can tell you once I threw out that belief, my speaking engagements improved and my reach and impact widened.

After one year at LSU, I left school because I thought I simply wasn't smart enough. This only served to reinforce the negative thoughts I carried around about my worth.

I was still having pain in my chest when I accepted a job offer to work at a large hospital in their Human Resources Department. After just two weeks I realized I'd made the biggest mistake of my life. I was experiencing what is referred to as the Peter Principle—that is, feeling I didn't know as much as the company thought I knew when they hired me. Also, my boss was asking us to do a secret project without the CEO of the hospital knowing about it.

Every night, I would wake up feeling as if there were an eight-hundred-pound elephant on my chest. I thought, "This is it, Linda. You're dying." I confided in a trusted friend, an RN, about what was happening to me, and she suggested I try hypnosis to let go of my stress. My first reaction was, "She's crazy to suggest something so out-there."

I left that job after two years and accepted a new position as an HR director at a home health agency. Two weeks into this job my boss called me into her office and said she wanted me to introduce a hypnotist who was coming in to educate the staff on the benefits of hypnosis.

The company had begun offering hypnosis to its patients, under doctor's orders, for pain management. I sat quietly and listened—with a healthy dose of skepticism—as the hypnotist spoke about what hypnosis is and isn't. The hypnotist did fun demonstrations that proved to me that our minds listen to our thoughts and try to make them true. That was a defining moment, when I first started to believe that maybe I could train my negative thoughts, this inner critic that beat me down all day every day, to become my best friend.

After the presentation my friend came over to me and said, "Linda, you need to learn how to practice self-hypnosis so that you can let go of your stress and relax. Hypnosis is a natural stress releasor." It all felt a little woo-woo to me, but I decided to give it a shot. When I told my husband about my pending appointment with the hypnotist, he said, "Oh, no. Don't go; they will brainwash you. You will never be the same." But at that point in my life, I was at a dead end and was willing to try anything to feel better.

Everything changed the day I first sat in Dr. Winkler's chair. As I listened to every word he said, I assumed that meant the hypnotism wasn't working. My inner critic woke up. "Shouldn't I be in a coma-like state? Linda, you're not even smart enough to let your-self be hypnotized."

I listened as my hypnotist gave me messages that I was self-confident, that I had a healthy self-esteem, that I could do anything I wanted. I listened and tried to stop thinking about what I would cook for dinner that night, while trying to ignore the thought telling me, "This is never going to work."

The more I listened to the hypnotist telling me I was loved and needed, the more I noticed my inner-critic voice getting quieter. When you're in a natural state of hypnosis, your inner critic (or Tasmanian Devil, as I call him) gets bored. Instead of rejecting those positive, affirming messages (as your Tasmanian Devil would do), your subconscious mind accepts them.

My Tasmanian Devil

I noticed my life starting to seriously change after just seventy-two hours. I started feeling better. I had more self-confidence and self-esteem. I was by no means "all fixed," but I could feel a difference in how I was thinking.

My hypnosis session had been so effective, I wanted to learn more about the universal laws of the mind.

The foundation of these laws can be summarized by these principles:

- Our thoughts are real and have significance.
- Thoughts are transmitted back and forth from us to others. They can hold us back or push us forward.
- Everything is energy and has a frequency, including our thoughts.
- Thoughts with emotions are attracted to other thoughts of the same emotion. We attract what we think about.
- We control what we think about. We can change our thoughts.

I signed up to attend a Saturday workshop Dr. Winkler was holding. I didn't have to tell Don I was going because a friend had invited him to go fishing. That was a God thing—He got Don out of the way so I could go. *Ha!* After that workshop I was hooked and signed up for the first course on how to become a certified hypnotist.

I remember telling Don what my plan was, and he sat looking at me like I was crazy. He never told any of his friends about my interest in hypnotism because he was hoping I would lose interest. Boy, was he wrong. I am still at it thirty years later and love every minute I spend helping people learn what I learned.

After completing the certification course, and armed with my newfound self-confidence, I decided it was time to make some changes in my professional life. In 1993, after spending seventeen years in the field of human resources, I gave up that high-paying job, a month's vacation, and a window office overlooking the Mississippi River in order to teach people about the power of the subconscious mind.

I quickly realized I could be the best hypnotist in the world, but if no one knew about me, my company would never be able to pay me a salary. So I was thrown feetfirst into marketing myself. I soon learned that in the business world, the fastest way to earning a significant income is either to double your rates, which I certainly could not do, or to start speaking. So that's what I did. I took any and every speaking opportunity I could. Baton Rouge, New Orleans, and Lafayette, Louisiana; San Antonio...I spoke and spoke and spoke.

I opened the Baton Rouge Hypnosis Clinic, and business was great! Money flowed in. My primary focus as a hypnotist was helping people lose weight. I had set out to develop a weight loss system that not only helped people lose weight but most importantly, helped people learn how to keep it off, and I had succeeded.

Fast-forward fifteen years. I didn't just learn to know, like, and respect myself. I was helping other people know me, like me, and respect me so they would want to do business with me and create a similar transformation in their own lives. This led to coauthoring the best seller *Answering the Call* with my friend and mentor Lisa Sasevich. Then, in 2014, I was thrilled to receive a Quilly Award for the book as well as an invitation to speak at the annual best-sellers summit in Hollywood.

Imagine me standing not in front of a group of college students but in front of hundreds of best-selling authors, experts, and entrepreneurs! It was such an honor to get to share my journey, my message, and my mission, but before I spoke, after the initial hit of adrenaline from what I was about to do wore off, a little alarm sounded in my brain that reminded me of my biggest fear. I was about to speak from the stage to a live audience.

I would not let this get the best of me. This wasn't my first rodeo; I had conquered this feeling before. So I asked myself this question: "Am I going to let my fear hold me back, or will I take a deep breath, brush the fear aside, and take the opportunity before me to talk about something I believe in?"

When I wrapped up my speech, I was shocked by the response. As I left the stage, fellow authors mobbed the stage, rushing to talk about something I'd said, to ask me a question, or just to give me a hug. I couldn't believe all the love that a roomful of strangers were willing to give this little girl from Baton Rouge!

When the crowds finally cleared, JW Dicks, cofounder of the National Academy of Best-Selling Authors, leaned over to me and said, "This is what you're meant to do."

He was right. This is why God put me through all the pain I've been through in my life. This is my purpose and my passion—helping to spread the word about how anyone can change their life without drugs and pills.

Scan QR code for video of me receiving the Quilly Award.

All these years later I've spoken to audiences from Hollywood to Palm Springs, California, to Canada. I was invited to speak at a Level Up event in Tallahassee for the Women's Prosperity Network. Thanks to the transformational work I have done, I sold over $11,000 in programs from the stage—just from speaking to a live audience in one short hour!

It has been such a wild, exciting, and beautiful ride. As I've discovered the power and strength of my own voice, I'm blessed to say that I've helped thousands of others do the same. Now I want to extend that same offer to you.

I've deliberately written this book in a conversational tone, as if I were sitting right in front of you, having private, one-on-one sessions. It's important that you feel as though I'm right there with you, walking you through each of the steps. Consider me your own personal coach assisting you in achieving your goals.

If you're in pain, that doesn't have to be your life. Don't stay stuck there. Or maybe you're thinking, "I already love, like, and respect myself. Why should I read this book?"

I wrote this book to help readers understand how their beliefs and habits are formed, how to command control of their thoughts, and ways to train their inner critic to be their best friend so they can become the captain of their own ship.

From this vantage point I can clearly see God's plan for my life. I'm writing this book at the tender age of eighty-three. It's my final offering before I officially and permanently retire. I never intended

to write a book, but God told me to write all this down so I could help people like you by sharing what I've learned along the way of my life's journey to happiness. He actually wouldn't leave me alone. Each morning for weeks He'd wake me at 5:30 and whisper that I needed to write down all I'd learned because He knew so many people who would be helped.

God is giving me peace about my choice to retire at this point, but only after I finish this one last thing: putting all I've learned in a book that others can read and be shown the path to happiness.

Before we continue, I want to address any feelings of apprehension you may have about the idea of hypnosis. Maybe it feels too far outside your comfort zone. As I mentioned, that was me too. But I can assure you, this book is full of statements backed by respected scientists, doctors, and psychologists who support using hypnotism as part of a comprehensive approach to mental health and well-being.

Hypnosis isn't something that's done *to* you. All hypnosis is *self-hypnosis*. Imagine the power of suggestion but on steroids. Simply put, hypnosis is the power of positive thinking, which can lead to happiness and fulfillment.

It may relieve you to know that I am a Christian and nothing I share runs contrary to my belief system. I consider myself a Christian hypnotist, but if you aren't a Christian, then when I use the term God, you can substitute that for whatever higher power you believe in.

One last thing before we begin: At the end of every chapter, which I call steps, you'll see a checklist of items to complete before moving on to the next chapter. It is very important that you not skip over this section. You may be asked to listen to a recording or write out answers to specific questions. The information and skills you will learn build on one another. If you skip an exercise, you miss out on getting the complete picture of how each step works and what it changes in your current mindset.

Additionally, each chapter has a "Roadmap to Success," a space to leave yourself notes. Don't be afraid to write in this book. Jot down what stuck out to you or statements you want to ponder later. Underline or highlight sentences that resonate with you. You might also want to keep a notebook and pen with you as you read.

This book is your tool, your guide, for achieving happiness in your life. If you only read the text and don't interact with it, you're doing yourself a disservice. At the end of the book I included a list of the resources available to you, should you want to continue learning about the methods described here.

At the end of every chapter you'll answer two questions:

1. What was my biggest takeaway from this chapter? Why?

2. What am I going to do today to be successful in achieving my goal?

Now look at what you wrote in your "Roadmap to Success" pages, and put it to use in achieving your goals.

You've already taken the hardest step in this entire process, which is acknowledging that you could be living a happier life. I will now coach you on how to transform your life using these five steps. I'll teach you how your beliefs are formed, how to control your thoughts, and how learning to practice self-hypnosis (a lifetime tool) can help you change your mindset so you can like, love, and respect yourself and truly believe the statement "I am good enough." It is time to stop giving away your power to others and find the happiness you deserve.

If I did it, so can you.

Here are a few suggestions you can check off to help you start thinking about areas you'd like to change:

- I would like to be happier.
- I would like to love myself more.
- I would like to eliminate negative thinking.

- I would like to learn to eat healthier.
- I would like to improve my sleep.
- I would like to have more self-confidence and self-esteem.
- I would like to reduce stress.
- I would like to reduce pain.
- I would like to eliminate headaches.
- I would like to improve my memory.
- I would like to train my inner critic to be my best friend.

Let's begin the journey.

PRELIMINARY WORK

S OME PEOPLE REFER to me as a "happiness coach." I love that title because happy is something we all want to be. Before we begin our work to achieve that goal, I have three action steps for you. You wouldn't go on a trip unless you had a map to get there, right? Consider this your roadmap to success.

To bring change into your life, you have to know exactly where you are. We'll be working together to help you find your starting point and then come up with a plan for where you're going.

The three steps are to complete the following:

1. Wheel of Life assessment

2. Stress Symptom checklist

3. A list of the ten most important people in your life

WHEEL OF LIFE

The Wheel of Life represents how you feel *overall* about your life at this moment in 12 Belief Change Life Categories.[1] These categories include how much money you make, your relationships, and your health. Areas you score low in indicate a logjam, which I will help you identify and unblock so that ultimately, you can find true happiness, health, and success.

WHEEL OF LIFE

Circle the number for how you feel about each of these areas of your life in the last month on a scale of 1 to 10, with 10 being the best. The definitions of these categories are on the next page.

Name: _____   Date: _____

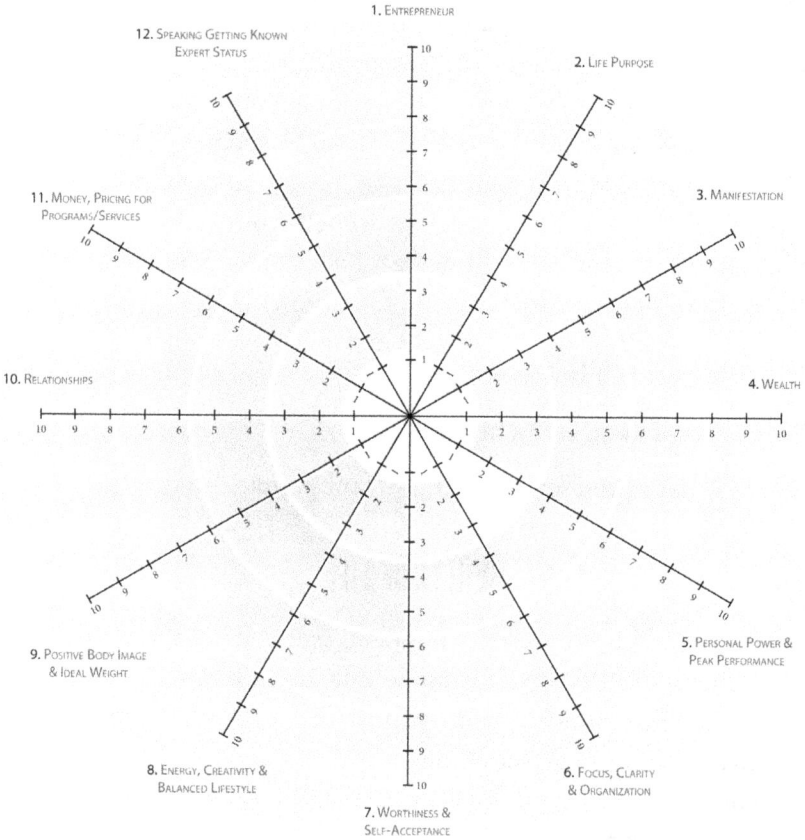

1. ENTREPRENEUR
2. LIFE PURPOSE
3. MANIFESTATION
4. WEALTH
5. PERSONAL POWER & PEAK PERFORMANCE
6. FOCUS, CLARITY & ORGANIZATION
7. WORTHINESS & SELF-ACCEPTANCE
8. ENERGY, CREATIVITY & BALANCED LIFESTYLE
9. POSITIVE BODY IMAGE & IDEAL WEIGHT
10. RELATIONSHIPS
11. MONEY, PRICING FOR PROGRAMS/SERVICES
12. SPEAKING GETTING KNOWN EXPERT STATUS

WHEEL OF LIFE DEFINITIONS

In my years of experience I feel in order to become successful in your business or life, you need to have the right mindset. There are hundreds of possible categories that limiting beliefs could fall into. I've narrowed the most popular beliefs down to the following twelve Belief Change Life Categories.

These twelve Belief Change Life Categories are based on the MindSonix Belief Change System. Together we will discover what your kingpin, or highest priority belief (HPB) is in each life category and help you break up your mental logjam and get rid of those negative beliefs to replace them with healthy, affirmative ones so you can continue on your journey to happiness.

Most of the twelve Belief Change Life Categories definitions on the Wheel of Life are self-explanatory, but there are a few (1, 3, and 4) that I feel need more clarification. Also, if you feel a category does not apply to you, just skip it.

1. Entrepreneur: Develop the right entrepreneurial mindset to succeed. If you are not an entrepreneur, and you work in a corporate environment or you don't work at all, just ask yourself this question: On a scale of 1 to 10, with 10 being the best, do I feel that I have developed the right mindset to succeed?

2. Life Purpose: Gain clarity about what you were meant to do with your life.

3. Manifestation: Become an unstoppable manifesting machine. We all have dreams and goals that sometimes we feel are way up in the sky, and we can't figure out how to bring these dreams and goals down into our physical world. After reflecting on what I just said, ask yourself this question: On a scale of 1 to 10, with 10 being the best, do I feel that I have become an unstoppable manifesting machine, and I am able to bring my dreams and goals into my physical world?

4. Wealth: Examine your feelings (negative and positive) about money. Ask yourself this question: On a scale of 1 to 10, with 10 being the best, after examining my feelings (negative and positive) about money, do I feel I am making the money I deserve?

5. Personal Power and Peak Performance: Have the confidence in yourself to do your best and be your best.

6. Focus, Clarity, and Organization: Stop procrastination in its tracks.

7. Worthiness and Self-Acceptance: Love and believe in yourself no matter what happens.

8. Energy, Creativity, and Balanced Lifestyle: Have the energy and inspiration to live the life you love.

9. Positive Body Image and Ideal Weight: Learn self-care, and to love, like, and respect yourself.

10. Relationships: Create healthy, positive dynamics and strong boundaries around all your relationships.

11. Money and Pricing for Programs/Services: Step into your power and charge what you are truly worth.

12. Speaking Getting Known and Expert Status: Feel your positive energy when your ideal clients and target audience know you are the "hottest ticket in town" and are eager to pay you for your services.

Keep in mind that you don't necessarily need to improve in each of these Belief Change Life Categories in order to benefit. However, in my experience, focusing on all of them to some extent gives you a better sense of well-being and helps you create amazing happiness, love, health, and prosperity. Change your mindset; change your life!

When you've finished, connect the circles on the wheel. Take a look at the shape and size of your wheel. Are you having a nice, smooth ride traveling down your life path, with every area in balance, or do you have a few flat spots that are making for a rough, bumpy ride? If everything was in balance in your life, you would have scored a minimum of 8, 9, or 10 in each area and your wheel would be large, round, and smooth.

Your lowest score is typically your biggest stressor. Would you agree? If your lowest score is in the Positive Body Image/Ideal Weight section, it reveals your true feelings, maybe something you've known but have been hiding from others, or maybe you've been hiding it from yourself too. Knowledge is power! We can't work on what we don't know is a problem. If you follow the suggestions I make in this book, you'll improve how you feel about your life—and in a relatively short period of time.

Don't panic if your wheel looks like a wet noodle instead of a smooth, wide-open circle. Do you remember when I told you about my inner critic and the green Tasmanian Devil that sat on my shoulder? That used to be my inner critic, and it prevented me from being who I truly am in my life, because I woke up every day thinking I was not good enough.

Take a look at the following two Wheel of Life examples. When they started the program, in September 2023, their wheel was much smaller. Just four weeks later, when they completed the program, in October 2023, it was much larger, which shows how much happier they are with their lives now that they are following my five-step surefire system to happiness.

BE THE HOTTEST TICKET IN TOWN
WHEEL-OF-LIFE

LINDA
ALLRED

CIRCLE THE NUMBER FOR HOW YOU FEEL ABOUT EACH OF THESE
AREAS OF YOUR LIFE ON A SCALE OF 1 TO 10 – 10 BEING THE "BEST!"

Name: Krista Wagner

10-01-2023
Date: 09-10-2023

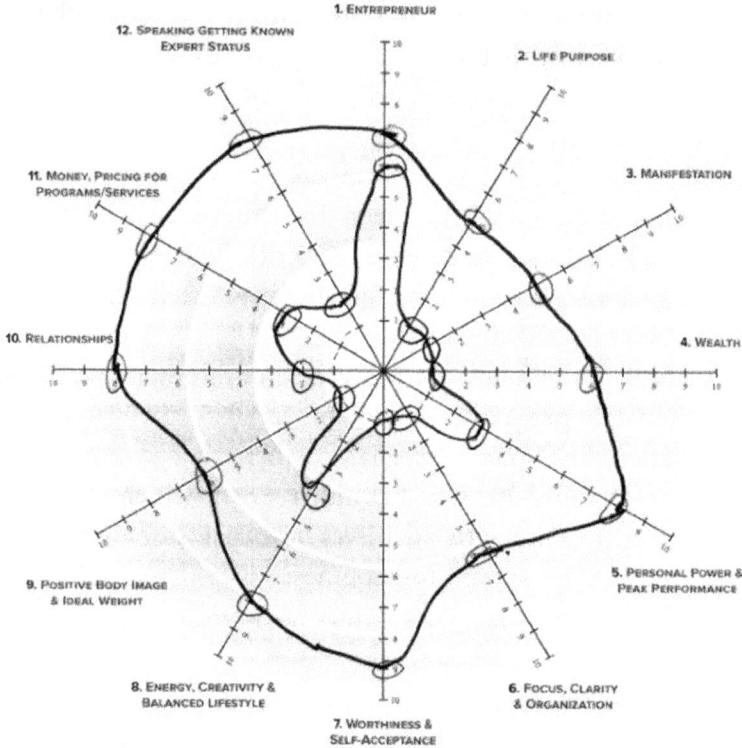

1. ENTREPRENEUR
12. SPEAKING GETTING KNOWN EXPERT STATUS
2. LIFE PURPOSE
11. MONEY, PRICING FOR PROGRAMS/SERVICES
3. MANIFESTATION
10. RELATIONSHIPS
4. WEALTH
9. POSITIVE BODY IMAGE & IDEAL WEIGHT
5. PERSONAL POWER & PEAK PERFORMANCE
8. ENERGY, CREATIVITY & BALANCED LIFESTYLE
6. FOCUS, CLARITY & ORGANIZATION
7. WORTHINESS & SELF-ACCEPTANCE

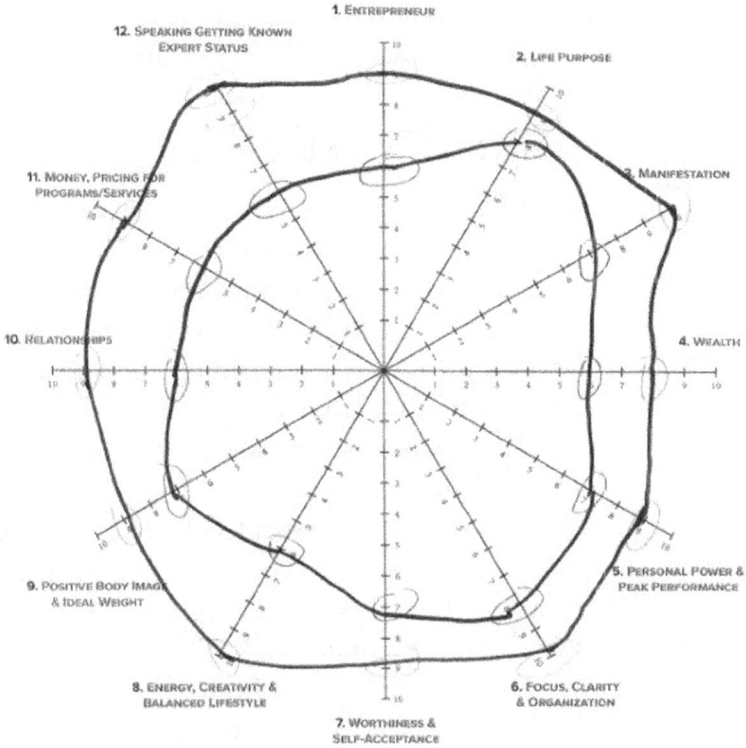

BE THE HOTTEST TICKET IN TOWN
WHEEL-OF-LIFE
CIRCLE THE NUMBER FOR HOW YOU FEEL ABOUT EACH OF THESE
AREAS OF YOUR LIFE ON A SCALE OF 1 TO 10 – 10 BEING THE "BEST!"

LINDA
ALLRED

Name: Kelsey Hann   Date: 09-13-2023

1. ENTREPRENEUR
12. SPEAKING GETTING KNOWN EXPERT STATUS
2. LIFE PURPOSE
11. MONEY, PRICING FOR PROGRAMS/SERVICES
3. MANIFESTATION
10. RELATIONSHIPS
4. WEALTH
9. POSITIVE BODY IMAGE & IDEAL WEIGHT
5. PERSONAL POWER & PEAK PERFORMANCE
8. ENERGY, CREATIVITY & BALANCED LIFESTYLE
6. FOCUS, CLARITY & ORGANIZATION
7. WORTHINESS & SELF-ACCEPTANCE

Maybe after seeing your Wheel of Life, you don't feel good enough, or smart enough, or healthy enough. And now you have evidence in the form of this wobbly wheel. Don't worry, we're going to do something about it. If you're not where you want to be, you will be; just stay with me.

Out of the twelve categories, maybe you're doing great in three areas. Then let's focus on the nine categories where you aren't where you want to be. Maybe that's why you go to sleep with a mind full of worry or stress, sleep fitfully or not enough, then wake up unhappy and slow to leave your bed the next morning. I want to help you increase all those categories so that you're living a balanced, full, and successful life. I want you to hop out of bed each morning with the eagerness of a new day and what lies ahead!

When you are underperforming or feel unsatisfied in areas of your life, it can result in mounting stress. Let's take a look at your stress level so we have a baseline of where you're starting.

STRESS SYMPTOM CHECKLIST

Have you ever wondered if your current problems have anything to do with how you are handling the current stress in your life? Could your stress level be associated with these problems?

Let me paint you a picture. When I first worked with my private clients, I described them as all wrapped up and twisted like a tight, thick rubber band. They carry all this stress and tension inside their bodies, and they don't know how to release it. They so desperately want to feel better. Can you relate?

Some turn to food to make themselves feel better; some reach out for alcohol or cigarettes or drugs. These things only mask or stuff down a person's emotions. Bad habits begin to form as they reach outside of themselves for comfort.

Learning to let go of your stress in a healthy, natural way by using positive affirmations or self-hypnosis will help you feel good about who you are. Then you won't need things outside of yourself to feel better. I learned to get high on life, with no pills, drugs, alcohol, cigarettes, or overeating, but simply by using the power of the mind God gave me and practicing self-hypnosis. I'll teach you how to do the same.

So, are you ready to take an honest look at your stress levels?

Check every symptom in this checklist if you have experienced it to a significant degree in the last month. Add up the two columns, and you will know instantly if you have low, moderate, high, or very high stress.

STRESS CHECKLIST

NAME: _____ DATE: _____

Instruction: Have you had any of these issues? Total the number of items checked.

Physical Issues

- ❑ Headaches (migraine or tension)
- ❑ Backaches
- ❑ Tight muscles
- ❑ Neck and shoulder pain
- ❑ Jaw tension
- ❑ Muscle cramps, spasms
- ❑ Nervous Stomach
- ❑ OTHER PAIN
- ❑ Nausea
- ❑ Insomnia (sleeping poorly)
- ❑ Fatigue, lack of energy
- ❑ High blood pressure
- ❑ Diarrhea
- ❑ Skin Condition (e.g., rash)
- ❑ Allergies
- ❑ Teeth grinding
- ❑ Digestive upsets (cramps, bloating)
- ❑ Heart beats rapidly or pounds, even at rest
- ❑ Stomach pain or ulcer
- ❑ Constipation
- ❑ Hypoglycemia
- ❑ Appetite change
- ❑ Colds
- ❑ Profuse perspiration
- ❑ Overeating
- ❑ Weight change
- ❑ When nervous, use of alcohol, cigarettes or recreational drugs

Psychological Issues

- ❑ Anxiety
- ❑ Depression
- ❑ Confusion or "spaciness"
- ❑ Irrational fears
- ❑ Compulsive behavior
- ❑ Forgetfulness
- ❑ Feeling "overloaded or overwhelmed"
- ❑ Hyperactivity – feeling you can't slow down
- ❑ Mood swings
- ❑ Loneliness
- ❑ Problems with relationships
- ❑ Dissatisfied/unhappy w/work
- ❑ Difficulty concentrating
- ❑ Frequent Irritability
- ❑ Restlessness
- ❑ Frequent boredom
- ❑ Frequent worrying / obsessing
- ❑ Frequent guilt
- ❑ Temper flare-ups
- ❑ Crying spells
- ❑ Nightmares

Evaluate your stress level as follows:

Total Checked: _____

Numbers of Items Checked	Stress Level
0-7	*Low*
8-14	*Moderate*
15-21	*High*
22+	*Very High*

Now I'd like you to think about the goals you want to accomplish. On the "Roadmap to Success" pages at the end of this chapter, list the primary goals you hope to achieve.

For example, I really don't advocate that you try to lose weight and stop smoking at the same time, as your subconscious mind will get confused. These types of goals need to be worked on separately. But along with wanting to lose weight or stop smoking, learning self-hypnosis can help you improve other areas of your life. So, what else would you like to achieve?

Also think about:

- What obstacles, challenges, and struggles do you regularly come up against?
- What would you like to see happen as a result of using this book? List everything you want to improve, change, or achieve in your life. For example, if you could walk into a "magic room" and could be transformed from the inside out—mind, body, and spirit—what are the end results you envision happening when you walk out of your "magic room"?
- How would these changes make a difference in your life?

These questions are also on the "Chapter Toolbox" page at the end of this chapter to allow you space to write down any specific responses you have to these questions. Remember that the goal of working together is to help you develop a different mindset, enrich your spirit, and enjoy your life. When your life is in balance and you learn to like, love, and respect yourself, you won't need food, alcohol, cigarettes, or drugs to feel better.

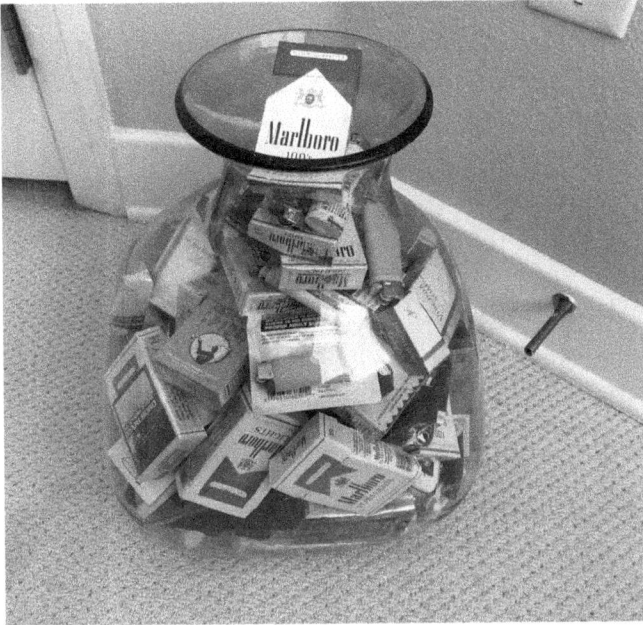

Clients gave me their cigarettes, indicating the clients' inner minds had confirmed they were now free from the smoking habit.

Often success is achieved once you learn to break bad habits. Just as important is becoming aware of what triggers you to turn to food, alcohol, cigarettes, or drugs for comfort. These are emotional responses and cause many people to binge when what they really want to do is drown out or escape from their emotional pain.

If you can learn to recognize the four trigger points that cause you to indulge in what I call emotional stress binges, you can reduce the number of times you automatically fall into this stress-binge trap.

Here are the four primary causes of emotional stress:

1. Life events and changes

2. Work or academic pressure

3. Relationship issues

4. Health challenges

The first step in reducing emotional stress is to recognize that you're even doing it in the first place. Once you learn how your emotions are controlling your bad stress binges, you can recognize the specific triggers that cause you to become unhappy. Then you find something healthier to do instead.

TEN MOST IMPORTANT PEOPLE IN YOUR LIFE

OK, now let's move to the last assessment, which requires you to think about the order of priorities in your life. Grab something to write with, and let's make a list.

Here, I want you to list the ten most important people in your life:

1.

2.

3.

4.

5.

6.

7.

8.

9.

10.

I hope it is clarifying to see the people you've listed. Now I have a question: Did you put yourself on the list?

Most of my clients fail to list themselves. If you didn't include yourself, I'd like you to think about why. Maybe it just didn't occur to you. Or maybe you think you aren't worth being in the top ten.

The order of priority ideally would look something like this:

1. God or your higher power

2. Yourself (If you're not happy, how can you share happiness with anyone else?)

3. Your family

4. Your job

God wants you to be happy and fulfilled, so it is OK to put yourself before your family. How can you give love to your family if you don't love yourself first?

When your Wheel of Life is in balance, you'll remember to put yourself near the top of the list because you'll have a growing sense of your self-worth.

After you have read this book and completed all the exercises, we'll do a program review, and you will *redo* the Wheel of Life and the Stress Symptom Checklist. You will have an opportunity to see how these stress symptoms start to disappear and how your Wheel of Life is getting rounder, bigger, and more balanced. I also recommend that you use a different-color pen to circle your new responses and write the new date on your sheet so you can see how practicing self-hypnosis and letting go of your stress in a healthy, natural way have made a difference in your life.

This exercise is an eye-opener and will show you very clearly how much your life has improved by incorporating these five steps as you walk toward reaching your full potential.

It is important that you not move forward to the next chapter until these three assessments are completed. If you are serious about overcoming your core blocks so you can have amazing results, it is critical to know your starting point.

I'm proud of you for putting effort into changing your life. Successful people never reach their goals on their own. Success comes when we surround ourselves with others who can support us along the way. Maybe it's a spouse, maybe it is a mentor—no matter who it is, we don't succeed alone. I'm honored to be coaching you on your journey to lasting happiness and transformation.

If you've bought this book and read this far, you've made one thing clear: You are more than just interested. Think of it this way: If you wanted to learn how to swim and you went to the swimming pool but would only ever dip a toe into the water, you may be showing interest, but it takes a lot more than that. It takes commitment. Positive life changes don't happen without commitment; they happen when you dive in and fully immerse yourself.

I speak from experience. I reached a point when my life was at an all-time low. I knew I couldn't stay there. I wanted more, and I wasn't getting any younger. I knew my life could be better and made the commitment to not give up until I believed I was worth it. So I gathered up all the courage I could muster, and I dove in. I learned everything I could to be happy, healthy, and successful. How about you? Are you ready to dive in?

If you're like me, it helps to know the lay of the land before you begin any journey. The five steps we'll be taking on our journey to find lasting happiness are as follows:

1. Understand Your Conscious and Subconscious Mind

2. Know the Benefits of Practicing Positive Self-Talk

3. Direct Your Mood Toward Happiness

4. Recognize Self-Hypnosis Is a Lifetime Tool

5. Get the Results You Want

These steps build on themselves, so it's important to go in order and read, watch, and listen to all the material I'll be providing.

If you wanted to build a two-story house, would you construct the second floor first? No, you'd build the ground level first, making sure the foundation was firm and durable. Well, this program is helping you build a solid foundation.

Step 1 begins with understanding your conscious and subconscious mind. You'll also learn about how kingpin beliefs can hold you back from finding true, lasting happiness.

Step 2 is about the benefits of practicing positive self-talk. Your subconscious makes up 95 percent of your mind. When you listen to supportive, positive messages, your subconscious mind will do everything within its power to make your thoughts come true. All of a sudden, you'll start feeling better because your mind is responding to positive suggestions instead of reacting to the inner critic, who is whispering, "You'll never be happy." This section also includes a QR code so you can listen to a positive-affirmation session, based on increasing self-confidence, one of the areas where almost everyone needs improvement.

The third step explains how to direct your mood toward happiness. You'll learn how to let go of your fears and anxieties by using a Willingness Mantra. The Willingness Mantra will become a guiding light when you experience daily challenges. You will also be introduced to the Joyometer, a powerful mood-management tool.

Step 4 tackles the topic of hypnosis. Hypnosis, at its core, uses the power of suggestion. I'll teach you how it works, give you some hypnosis tools, and include a QR code so you can listen to a couple of my favorite self-hypnotizing sessions designed to reduce stress, experience peace, and increase happiness and well-being.

The final step of the journey to lasting happiness is a practical guide to getting the results you want using a more involved explanation of habits, knowledge of the importance of breaking bad habits, and tools to continue targeting the areas where you still need work. The book is full of free downloads and resources to help you succeed.

One last thing before we dive in. I want you to think back to your Wheel of Life. There are likely a number of areas that could stand improvement in your overall plan for increased happiness, health, and success. I want you to choose one area to work on first.

Next, visualize what success would look like in that category.

Now, flip ahead a couple of pages until you see the "Roadmap for Success" page.

In response to the question "What am I going to do today to be successful in achieving my goals?" I'd like you to list the first goal you want to tackle, along with steps you intend to take to get started.

Put your goal in a place where you'll see it first thing after you wake up. Maybe that's on the calendar on your phone or an index card by your bedside. Just make sure your eyes land on this before you get out of bed.

Then, as part of your practical plan to achieve your day's goal, look over your "Roadmap to Success" pages each and every day. Include notes on material that you found helpful or that you wanted to spend more time thinking about. Pick one or two things to do that day that will help you stay on track toward hitting the goal.

As you continue through the book, be generous with your notes, knowing you'll go back to these to form your plan for achieving whatever goal you're working on.

From this moment forward you never, never, never have permission to put your feet on the floor in the morning until you ask yourself your Commitment Question: *What am I going to do today to be successful in achieving my goals in [this one area]?* As an added motivator, sign the Responsibility Contract to remind you that achieving your goal is your responsibility!

RESPONSIBILITY CONTRACT

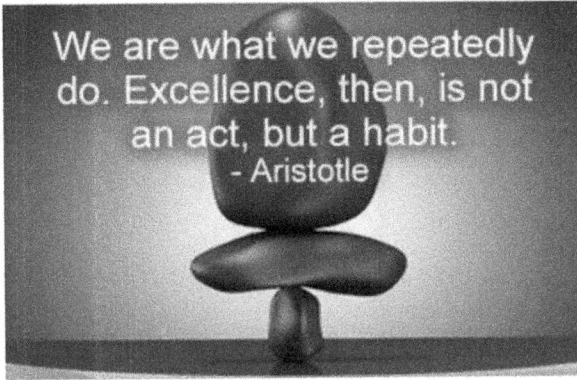

We are what we repeatedly do. Excellence, then, is not an act, but a habit.
- Aristotle

I UNDERSTAND THAT ACHIEVING MY GOAL IS MY RESPONSIBILITY.

NAME _____   DATE _____

As we move through the chapters and review the tools learned, look over the notes you've written on the "Roadmap to Success" pages to help you stay excited and motivated toward achieving your goals.

CHAPTER TOOLBOX

Complete Assessments:

- Wheel of Life _____
- Stress Symptom Checklist _____
- 10 Most Important People in Your Life _____

Select the first category you want to improve. Visualize what success looks like in this category.

_____

_____

_____

_____

List the primary goals you hope to achieve in each area that you scored less than 8:

_____

_____

_____

_____

_____

_____

_____

_____

_____

What obstacles, challenges, and struggles do you regularly come up against when deciding to achieve a goal or quit a bad habit?

_____

_____

_____

_____

_____

_____

_____

What would you like to see happen as a result of using this book? List everything you want to improve, change, or achieve in your life. For example, if you could walk into a "magic room" and be transformed from the inside out—mind, body, and spirit—what are the end results you envision happening when you walk out of your "magic room?")

_____

_____

_____

_____

_____

_____

_____

_____

How would these changes make a difference in your life?

_____

_____

_____

_____

_____

_____

_____

_____

_____

Sign the Responsibility Contract _____

ROADMAP TO SUCCESS

You do not have permission to get out of bed in the morning until you ask yourself this question: What am I going to do today to be successful in achieving my goal?

1.

_____

_____

_____

2.

_____

_____

_____

3.

_____

_____

_____

4.

_____

_____

_____

5.

_____

_____

_____

6.

7.

8.

9.

10.

Step 1

UNDERSTAND YOUR CONSCIOUS AND SUBCONSCIOUS MIND

YOU COULD BE a musical protégé, an Olympic-ready athlete, a creative genius, or the most driven and motivated professional in your field. Here is the door of opportunity. You dream of walking through it. Maybe you want to lose weight, stop smoking, make more money, be in a loving relationship, or reduce stress, anxiety, and fear. So what is holding you back from walking through the door?

One thing stands in your way. If not dealt with or managed well, this one thing will threaten your chances of success and keep you from achieving your true potential, no matter how much time, effort, and energy you've invested.

It took me many, many years to discover this one thing and learn how to remove it from my life, once and for all. Thirty years later I've built the business of my dreams, and I'm the happiest and healthiest I've ever been. I've helped thousands of men and women just like you find the same kind of freedom and success in their own lives. I want to help you uncover the one thing holding you back so that you can finally have the personal, professional, or financial success you deserve.

Now, before we go any further, I want to share a bit about myself and some of the early events in my life that shaped the way I view myself. As I said earlier, I didn't grow up in poverty, and I wasn't physically abused. But I did grow up with an alcoholic father who ignored me. I spent the first decades of my life thinking I was inadequate. When I was a teenager, my mother told me, "You don't have to go to college. You find a man who has a degree who will support you. Don't argue. Keep the peace, and keep your mouth shut."

I fell in love, or puppy love, with my husband, Don, when I was in middle school. I thought he was so handsome. He asked me out when I was a sophomore in high school, and I married him when I was seventeen going on eighteen years old. He was two years older than me, and he talked to me, as you know, and my dad ignored me, so Don made me feel special.

On my wedding night, after putting on my bridal nightgown, I walked into the bedroom to find my husband standing by the bed. He said, "Come here." On the bed he had laid a pair of pants. "We have to decide right now who is going to wear the pants in the family—you or me."

I was completely confused, so he repeated himself. Being a shy, immature seventeen-year-old girl, I said, "Darling, you are."

And so began the path of my husband controlling every aspect of my life. The flip side of this was I was too chicken to be outspoken. There were things I liked and did not like about Don too, but because my mom, whom I love dearly and who is now passed, said, "Linda, if you cannot say something nice about someone, then don't say anything at all," I kept my mouth shut.

I worked two jobs to help pay our bills while Don went to college. We hadn't been married too long before Don began calling me stupid. No matter what I did or didn't do, I could never please him. I could set a perfect dinner table, and he would put me down because I'd forgotten to put the saltshaker on the table.

When someone whom you love and respect repeatedly calls you dumb and stupid, you begin to believe it must be true. This is when I began to believe that I was not good enough. I also felt inferior because all our friends (all Don's friends) were college educated. I can still hear my mother saying, "Linda, the man is the head of the family. Don't talk back to him. Try to keep him happy."

Years later he followed the same pattern when our boys were growing up, criticizing everything they did. In retrospect this was his way of making himself feel good. By putting other people down, it made him feel important. My journey to prove to my husband that I was good enough began very early in my marriage.

Meanwhile, what happened to who Linda was? What happened to what Linda wanted? After years of being afraid to speak up because Linda was supposed to be a "good little girl" and stuff down all her feelings and not tell her husband how she felt, I started overeating to cover up my hurt. I became the best doormat in the world, and if Don or anyone else in my world said something to hurt my feelings, I would just sweep those hurts under the rug, smile, tell myself, "Everything is OK," and go on with life.

This led to my emotional eating and creating a forty-pound overweight problem, which eventually led to me specializing in weight loss, writing the *Weight Off NOW! Get Healthy—Get Happy Self-Hypnosis Home Study System*. But it was many years before all this would come about.

I became a workaholic to prove that I wasn't dumb and that I wasn't a failure. I was determined to succeed. But when I'd get accolades or praise for my work, my inner critic was quick to reject any positive messages. That (Tasmanian) devil sitting on my shoulder sabotaged any efforts to see myself in a positive light— that is, of course, until I tried hypnosis and discovered what was holding me back from true freedom and a successful life. This one thing stood in my way and kept me from reaching my fullest potential and living a successful, fruitful, and productive life.

With every client I work with, any problems they have can be tied to this one thing—and the one thing is different for each person. Whether it affects their career, relationships, or physical health and well-being, this one thing seems like an impossible burden to remove. But removing it is much easier than it seems. And once you discover what this one thing is and how you can control the role it plays in your life, there are no limits to what you can achieve.

YOUR KINGPIN BELIEF

A few years ago I was invited to have lunch with a friend so she could bounce a few business strategy ideas off me. We talked for almost two hours about ways to cut costs, increase her profits, and create new systems for her business that would bring her huge gains for years to come.

A good hour into the discussion, after working out an entirely new plan, she looked at me and said, "You know what, Linda? I really believe in my business, and I believe I could make at least $100,000 a year or more if I put into action everything we talked about doing" (insert dramatic music here).

"But in the back of my mind, there is always the same thought that continues to haunt me: What if I just don't deserve all this money?"

Now, you might say this is just part and parcel to being a woman. Theatlantic.com reported in 2014 that women are still far less self-assured and less confident pursuing their business goals and dreams compared with men.[1]

However, the "one thing" I am referring to goes far beyond gender lines and affects all ethnic, religious, and socioeconomic backgrounds. I call it the "kingpin belief," and it is what's standing in the way of your success.

To help you understand how it works, let me paint you a picture. Imagine a river in which loggers are transporting timber. As the water flows and the logs float along, from time to time they get jammed. When this happens, a very sudden and tangible change occurs. The flow of the water stops completely. Nothing moves. This is obviously a problem for the loggers, who need a steady stream of water to move their supply and finish the job. How do they solve this problem?

The most common and obvious answer is, "Move the logs out of the way, one at a time, of course!" The true solution, however, takes much less effort and is simpler than you might believe. In order for the loggers to get the water flowing again, all they have to do is look for the key log, or "kingpin" (the one log that started the jam in the first place) that is holding all the other logs frozen in place. Once the "kingpin" log is removed, the water will be freed and continue to flow again.

My friend was revealing to me her kingpin log ("What if I just don't deserve all this money?"), the one thing holding back her success, no matter what she tried. She recognized that she was stuck and wanted to understand it.

In the same way, we all have mental kingpins, or limiting beliefs, that are standing in the way of all our power, gifts, and potential. To get a full picture of how our successes are connected to our beliefs, we need a better understanding of how the mind works.

MANIFESTATION FORMULA

Let's begin with a simple equation. This manifestation formula (created by Nikkea B. Devida in her MindSonix™ program) is your ticket to understanding how you can meet your goals as well as identifying what might be keeping you stuck.

Beliefs + Thoughts + Feelings + Actions = Results

We all have dreams and goals that float around in our imagination, but we may not have found a way to bring those dreams and goals into the physical world. I'll make the bold claim that once you understand this manifestation formula, you'll be well on your way to having those dreams become a reality.

Your beliefs lead to your thoughts, your thoughts lead to your feelings, your feelings lead to your actions, and your actions lead to your results. So if you're not getting the results you want, step back one and look at your actions. If you're not taking the actions every day to get the results that you want, why aren't you?

If you can't answer that question, take one step back and look at your feelings. What feelings do you have about achieving your goals? Are they positive or negative?

If your feelings are negative, take one step back and look at your thoughts. What are your thoughts regarding your ability to accomplish your goals? Do you have doubts? Where are those doubts coming from?

If your thoughts are negative, move back one more step to the beginning of the formula, and look at your beliefs. What limiting beliefs, or kingpins, are holding you back from taking actions every day to get the results you want? Not sure? Let's take a look again at your Wheel of Life.

In what areas did you score the lowest? Those are where your most limiting beliefs reside. Until these beliefs are addressed and corrected, you will struggle to achieve success. Would you believe me if I told you that you can change your beliefs by tapping into your subconscious mind? Let me tell you about the Louisiana Weight Loss Challenge.

As I've already mentioned, I put together a weight loss system called *Weight Off NOW! Get Healthy—Get Happy Self-Hypnosis Home Study System.* I knew a lot about weight loss, as I personally struggled to lose those forty pounds I'd put on from being a comfort eater. I am happy to say that I did lose those pesky pounds using hypnosis and have kept it off for over thirty years now.

After I published the system, I got the idea to do a Louisiana Weight Loss Challenge. I chose six ladies to use my home study system to prove that you did not have to go see a hypnosis live and in person but could instead listen to hypnosis sessions in the privacy of your own home.

To be considered, each potential candidate wrote me an essay about why I should choose them as one of the six ladies. Wow! I had hundreds of email essays come in. The local TV media found out about the challenge and interviewed one of the six ladies each month to see how they were doing and to show their progress. They also filmed the ceremony when I announced the winner.

Meredith Eicher won the challenge. I'd like to share her initial essay so you can see where she was mentally and physically before the challenge began.

Meredith's before picture

I was born fat. I am the successful business owner, out-standing member/president of almost every activity I have ever been involved in since I can remember. However, I am a failure at controlling my weight. I am the healthiest fat girl you will ever meet and a Pennington workup substanti-ates that comment. I have tried every weight loss fad, from Optifast to the cabbage soup diet—you can't name one that I have not tried. I thought fen-phen was great even knowing it could kill me. At least I would die skinny.

I am approaching 50 (my mom died at 50), and every day I look in the mirror and struggle. Everyone in business and my personal life thinks that I am a confident person. If they only knew that I struggle each and every day with my appearance…I never again want to hear these words: "She has such a beautiful face and eyes." I really need to enter this challenge and get my life back.

Meredith's after picture

Here's what she had to say after completing the Louisiana Weight Loss Challenge:

> This journey has truly transformed my life. The first and foremost insight was the realization that the stress of my everyday life, from professional obligations to family and personal obligations, drives me to seek comfort in food. The *Weight Off NOW! [Get Healthy—Get Happy] Self-Hypnosis Home Study System*™ manual's approach encouraged me to look back to when I first used food as a comfort, and I discovered that I developed this habit as a reward for pleasing others.
>
> When I completed a task, which my inner voice usually had me worked up into a major stress level, I rewarded myself with food. The trend followed into my adulthood but at a more intense level due to the increased stress that balancing work and personal life brings.
>
> Linda's program first made me aware of the issue, and then I took a systematic approach to the beginning of my transformation. I learned to reduce my stress by way of hypnosis and to change my subconscious thoughts and behaviors by way of hypnosis and positive thinking. Once I adopted this new way of thinking, the rest of the program was simple.
>
> I learned that habits can be changed if and only if I was willing to visualize and be open to the possibilities. Habits and my inner voice have been retrained as a result. I recognize that the continued use of the [recordings] will keep old habits and my "inner critic" from returning. All of this takes the focus off of using food as a reward. Therefore, eating is used to sustain myself, not to reward myself for a good deed.
>
> The nutrition and exercise education part of the program I had heard over the years, but had failed to listen. However, since Linda took me to a place where I no longer needed food as a reward, making healthy choices became simple. In the past, my changes hadn't been internal. Losing weight meant being on a "diet." I would lose some weight, then turn around and eat whatever I wanted...again. Over and over.
>
> So far, I've lost 25 pounds, 3 dress sizes, and 2 pant sizes,

along with 21 inches in total. My new positive thinking and relaxed feelings drove me to exercise even more. My inner voice is now positive and free of guilt. The amazing part of this experience was never feeling like I was on a diet and I never once fought myself at the table. The change in my eating habits was natural. This program will be in my life forever. Thanks, Linda!

—MEREDITH EICHER

I'm still so proud of Meredith and all six participants. Congratulations again, Meredith, on your achievement! Meredith mentioned the internal changes she made, much of which regarded the conscious and subconscious minds, so let's take a closer look there.

THE CONSCIOUS AND SUBCONSCIOUS MIND

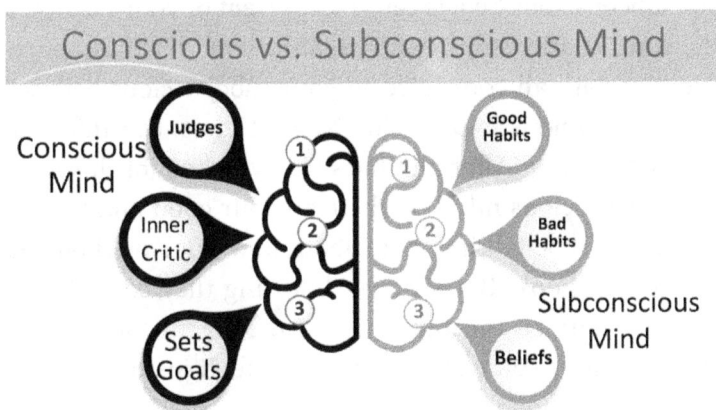

Our minds are divided into two levels: conscious and subconscious. Your conscious mind makes judgments, such as 2 + 2 = 4. The conscious mind is also where your inner critic lives and where we set goals for ourselves. If you're reading this book, then you have a goal you want to achieve.

Five percent of your mind is conscious—the other 95 percent is your subconscious.[2] If you've been trying to achieve your goals using 5 percent of your conscious mind, no wonder you're struggling to find success. So how do we tap into the other 95 percent?

When you were in school, I bet you never heard a teacher say we have power over our subconscious mind. Am I right? I never even heard the term *subconscious mind* when I was in school. But science has a great deal to say about this. Dr. Bruce Lipton, a cellular biologist known for his research on the body-mind connection, wrote, "The moment you change your perception is the moment you rewrite the chemistry of your body."[3]

Gaining control of your subconscious mind is the one thing we all must master; otherwise we stay stuck in our limiting beliefs—confused, spinning our wheels but going nowhere. So let me say this again: Your beliefs lead to your thoughts, your thoughts lead to your feelings, your feelings lead to your actions, and all these combined equal your results, which then become habits and behaviors.

Your subconscious beliefs cause 95 percent of your results. Your health, your relationships, your wealth, your business purpose, your success—it's all connected to your subconscious beliefs. The subconscious mind is so powerful. Now let's turn this information into transformation. After all, that's why you bought this book!

Your subconscious mind is where all your good and bad habits are stored. We'll be talking more about how influential our habits are later in the book. But for now, knowing they come from our subconscious mind is the important part. Your subconscious mind does not care how you want to live your life. It just listens to your beliefs and your thoughts.

Let's have some fun and do a little demonstration so I can show you how your mind listens to your thoughts. You need to be in a quiet environment where you won't be disturbed.

Now, what just happened? You knew you didn't have heavy sacks on your eyes. But do you see how your mind accepted the suggestion and made your thoughts real? Imagine what your

Scan QR code for a "heavy sacks on your eyes" demonstration.

subconscious believes when all it hears is "I'm so dumb. I'm a failure. I can't quit smoking." Now imagine the changes to your life if instead you told yourself, "I am smart. I am successful. I can do anything I put my mind to."

Now, indulge me here. I would like you to take a deep, deep breath because I never ever want you to forget this. Your subconscious mind, which makes up 95 percent of your mind, does *not* care how you want to live your life; it just listens, listens, listens to your conscious thoughts and then does everything within its power to make your conscious thoughts true.

Try this: Every time you have a negative thought, tell yourself, "I need to turn that negative thought into a positive thought because my mind doesn't care. It's just listening and trying everything within its power to make my thoughts true. I have a choice. I can be happy or sad. It's up to me." You have control over your thoughts! Why choose sad?

OK, let's move on to how each of these levels in your mind understands time. The conscious mind understands linear time— past, present, and future. However, your subconscious mind understands only present time.

There's also an area of study called genomic imprinting that suggests that three months *before* our conception our beliefs are downloaded. Lipton has studied how environmental influences, including parental beliefs and experiences, can impact gene expression and the development of a person even before their conception.

Think of it as getting a jump start on our beliefs from our great-grandparents, our grandparents, and our parents. It's not until we're about ten or eleven years old that we can begin to question where our beliefs come from and what we process, what we want to hold on to, and what we'd rather get rid of.

Part of the biological download includes programming a person to survive. As adults we realize that surviving doesn't always equal having a happy life. Thriving comes when we can walk through that door of opportunity and achieve our dreams.

Another key aspect of the two levels of the mind concerns the speed at which they process information. The conscious mind processes information at forty to fifty bits of information a second; the subconscious, eleven billion bits per second.[4] This shows you just how much more your subconscious mind is taking in. Both are very powerful, but they are also very different.

Think of it like this: Imagine you walked out in the backyard on a clear night, looked up at the sky, and could see only one star. That one star represents the power on your conscious mind. Now imagine the night sky as it is. All the other stars that you can see, and even the ones you cannot see, represent the power of your subconscious.

I hope you're beginning to see why it's so important for your subconscious beliefs to reflect your conscious beliefs in your future success. Do not listen when your inner critic tries to run you down with negative thoughts. Your feelings and beliefs are controlled by your subconscious mind.

Now I hope you're beginning to understand how your kingpin belief is holding you back and how important it is to dislodge it. In the following chapters I'll share some principles on how your subconscious mind can dislodge your kingpin so you can find true success.

As I said earlier, your subconscious mind doesn't care about you or your hopes, dreams, and goals. It only listens to your thoughts and does everything it can to make your thoughts true for you. In much the same way, your thoughts are like a thermostat. Let's say you set your thermostat for seventy-two degrees. It is designed to turn on when the temperature of the room raises above seventy-two degrees, and it runs until seventy-two degrees becomes the temperature again. It cannot do more or less than it's programmed for. This is how our minds work too. We tell ourselves what we believe. "I think I can make $50K a year, but I could never make $100K." What would happen if you let go of those beliefs? Change the temperature on your thermostat if you aren't happy with how the room feels.

Another way to say this is, you need to fix your stinkin' thinkin'! Once your mind is set to the right "temperature," your body (or actions) will have no choice but to fall in line. Then, there will be no limit to what you can achieve.

If you know right now there's a logjam, or kingpin, holding you back from success, I want to show you how to find it and get it out of your life, once and for all. You can learn to reprogram your subconscious beliefs.

NEUROPLASTICITY

Maybe you're thinking, "I'm too old," or, "I'm too set in my ways to change." One of the breakthroughs of the century came with the discovery of neuroplasticity. The general understanding until this breakthrough was that our minds weren't adaptable. But it turns out our thinking is more pliable than we realized.

Dr. Caroline Leaf wrote in her book *Switch on Your Brain*, "Thoughts are real, physical things that occupy mental real estate. Moment by moment, every day, you are changing the structure of your brain through your thinking. When we hope, it is an activity of the mind that changes the structure of our brain in a positive and normal direction."[5]

Since the brain is the computer and our thoughts the software, we can reprogram our subconscious beliefs and change our stinkin' thinkin'. Our beliefs aren't hardwired; we have the power to change them! Knowing you can program your mind to believe that you are capable of so much more, are you feeling more inspired to walk through that door of opportunity?

When you look in the mirror, do you see a little kitty cat afraid of its shadow? Or do you see a lion, fierce and majestic? By the time you finish this book, you'll have a better understanding of what you believe and don't believe about yourself. Are you ready to get rid of your kingpin and stand before a mirror as the king of the jungle? Go ahead, start working on your roar.

A kitten was always staring back at me. I had a long way to go to get to the woman I am today. So for anybody reading this, feeling like you don't have the strength to climb the hill in front of you, let me tell you, you think you don't have control of your life, but you do. It starts with you believing it.

Remember, your subconscious beliefs drive the results you get. Those beliefs are the foundation of what you think, what you think is the foundation of what you feel, what you feel determines what actions you'll take, and those actions lead to the results you'll get.

I want to share one more story with you before we move on to step 2. Years ago I had a client enroll in my Stress Management Program. She was a kindergarten teacher who had two more years before she could retire. However, she had severe arthritis, and when she got down on the floor to play with her students, she was in so much pain she could hardly get back up.

I told her I was going to teach her Creative Visualization (CV), which is a technique where the person makes believe, imagines, or pretends in their mind that they are achieving their most sought-after goal. CV is another term for self-hypnosis.

I told her to visualize the outcome she hoped to achieve and to intentionally practice Creative Visualization every night as she was falling asleep and every morning right as she was waking up. I then told her to close her eyes and imagine she was living her best life—to imagine being pain-free, doing all the activities she wanted to do, playing on the floor with her kindergarten students, and getting up quickly with no pain or stiffness. She could walk outside and look at the beautiful blue sky and sunshine, go shopping, eat out with friends. I told her to see herself smiling and happy, enjoying her life. "I want you to practice this exercise every day."

She looked at me like I was crazy and said, "Linda, I have to hold on to the dresser in my bedroom to get to the bathroom every morning because I am in so much pain."

I shrugged. "What do you have to lose?"

I will never forget what happened next. The following week when she came in for her appointment, she stood half in the hall and half in my office.

I said, "Hello! Come on in!"

She immediately put her hand on her hip and in a loud, confident voice said, "Linda, you know I am a teacher, and teachers are always right. That crazy visualization thing you wanted me to do imagining I was pain-free?"

"Yes," I said.

"Well, I just had the best week of my life. I cannot believe that just by changing my focus away from how much pain I was in, to positive, uplifting thoughts could make such a difference. Thank you so much!"

When we shift our focus from negative to positive, we change our thoughts, our feelings, and our actions. The more detailed your visualization, the more success you'll have—i.e., "What do I see? What do I smell? What do I taste? What do I hear? What do I feel?" Do this every day, and watch while your dreams start coming true.

Before we move on to the next topic, I want to share with you my personal guiding principle—I heard the motivational speaker, author, and entrepreneur Jim Rohn say it: "I am willing to do today what most people won't because tomorrow I will have what most people won't."

You've stepped up to the plate. You know what they say: "If you want to know what your life will look like in five years, just keep doing the same thing." I know you're tired. But I believe you are willing to do whatever it takes to reprogram your mind and leave these heavy-burdened days behind.

Your final task before moving to the next chapter is to listen to the meditation "The Greatest Secret." Here, I've included the transcript of the first few minutes, but click on the QR code to listen to the complete MP3.

Don't forget to jot down on your Roadmap to Success pages the statements you want to revisit later.

THE GREATEST SECRET

The following story is an oriental fable about ancient gods who were trying to decide where to hide the greatest power in the universe so humankind would not be able to find it and use it destructively.

"I am willing to do today what most people won't because tomorrow I will have what most people won't."

One of the gods said, "Let's hide it on the top of the highest mountain." They discussed that idea and decided that would not do because humans would eventually climb the highest mountain and find that great power.

"The Greatest Secret"

A second god came up with the idea of hiding the greatest power at the bottom of the ocean, and after another discussion, they decided that humans would eventually figure out a way to investigate the bottom of the ocean.

When you're ready, let's continue to step 2.

STEP 1 CHAPTER TOOLBOX

What is the biggest takeaway from this chapter? Why?

_____

_____

_____

_____

_____

_____

Look at what you wrote on the "Roadmap to Success" pages in the previous session. Do you see changes in the area you're working on? Record those here.

_____

_____

_____

_____

_____

_____

_____

_____

_____

_____

STEP 1
ROADMAP TO SUCCESS

What am I going to do today to be successful in achieving my goal?

1.

_____

_____

_____

2.

_____

_____

_____

3.

_____

_____

_____

4.

_____

_____

_____

5.

_____

_____

_____

6.

7.

8.

9.

10.

Step 2

KNOW THE BENEFITS OF PRACTICING POSITIVE SELF-TALK

HAD A CLIENT who was a kindergarten teacher, and one day she was telling me about her students. "It seems impossible to get them to take an afternoon nap! They giggle; they won't lie still; they get into little fights with each other. It's a mess, and I don't know how to control them."

"I can fix this," I told her.

"How?"

"Play my positive affirmation (PA) session, 'Child's Health and Confidence' (made for children under eleven years old) when they lie down to go to sleep."

She said she was willing to give it a try. A week or so later, when she came in for her next session, she said, "Linda, the first time I played the PA at the start of nap time, they all looked at me strangely; then they giggled and still acted out some. However, the next day, I played it again, and they all got quiet and didn't say much but still did not go to sleep. The following day, I decided not to play it, and all of a sudden, one of the students piped up, "Why aren't you playing what that nice lady says?" and I heard the others around the room say, "Yes, please play it!"

"From that day on, I played the PA, and they all got quiet and went right to sleep every day when nap time came. Linda, thank you so much."

The key to success is learning how to reprogram your thoughts, whether it's silencing your inner critic that tries to convince you that you are not good enough, or it's stopping a behavior that is unhealthy. Change the way you think, and you'll change the way you act.

In step 1 you were introduced to the manifestation formula that shows how your beliefs lead to your thoughts, your thoughts lead to your feelings, your feelings lead to your actions, and your actions lead to results. So if you're not achieving the goals you want, back up a step. Are you taking action every day to achieve those results? Why not? What limiting beliefs are holding you back from taking those actions?

We've also done the Wheel of Life exercise to identify in what areas you score the lowest. Your lowest scores indicate areas where you have the most limiting beliefs, or kingpins, holding you back.

OK, let's jump into step 2, where we can take this information and turn it into lasting transformation. I want to talk about the power of two little words:

I am.

They look fairly simple on the page, right? Let me help you understand just why they are so powerful.

When you say, "I am stupid," you immediately *feel* stupid. When you say, "I am intelligent," you feel intelligent. Your subconscious takes the thoughts you feed it and tries to make them true. Remember, your subconscious makes up 95 percent of your mind and does not care how you want to live your life. It just listens, listens, listens to your conscious thoughts and does everything within its power to make these thoughts true for you.

In step 1, I explained how the conscious mind understands linear time—past, present, and future. But the subconscious mind understands only present time. When we speak to ourselves, we use present tense:

I am successful.

I am a nonsmoker.

I am healthy.

I am making all the money I choose to make.

I am in the perfect relationship.

The subconscious mind does everything within its power to make these thoughts true for you. This is why I can say with complete confidence that you may think you don't have control over your life, but you are in absolute control. You can wake up and choose to be happy, or you can wake up and choose to be sad—your subconscious doesn't care. It just listens to your thoughts.

Our minds are most receptive to these statements when we're in a dreamlike state, like as we fall asleep or as we're waking up. Those are the best times to offer yourself positive affirmations.

We also discussed in step 1 the idea of genomic imprinting and how scientists are researching how our beliefs are downloaded three months before our conception. But because of the discovery of neuroplasticity, the brain can change. If your mind is a computer, your thoughts have programmed your mind to believe certain things. The software that's running on your computer is your stinkin' thinkin' or your good thinking. All you have to do to change the outcome is reprogram the input. That's what these five steps are teaching you to do—to reprogram your subconscious mind.

Now let's talk about the hypnosis demonstration you did in step 1. (If you didn't listen to that recording, stop here and go do that. To achieve the success you're looking for, you have to complete these steps in order, which includes the activities). I asked you to close your eyes and make believe that you had fifty-pound sacks on your eyes.

The subconscious loves to make believe, imagine, and pretend. You knew you did not have heavy sacks on your eyes, but your mind acted as if it were true. You were thinking it, and it did everything within its power to make your thoughts true. Remember this activity anytime you have a negative thought such as "I am stupid," and immediately reverse it by telling yourself, "I am intelligent."

You will learn, day by day, to listen more closely to your inner thoughts. When you hear a thought that is not helping you hit your goal, then catch it and say, "OK, what do I need to tell myself to help me move closer toward my goals?" You can learn to make your inner critic your best friend.

MY CLOSET STORY

When I was compensation manager at the hospital where I worked, my password on my computer was "Serenity" because I felt if I ever found serenity, I must be dead and in heaven.

To illustrate how desperate I was to change my stinkin' thinkin', let me tell you this crazy story. I had a large carpeted office with a huge walk-in closet. I had an hour for lunch, and every day, I made a habit of eating at my desk. Then I would go into my closet and listen to a self-hypnosis or a positive affirmations cassette on my tape recorder. (No CDs back then and not many options to listen to cassettes unobtrusively!)

I would bring a flashlight with me because guess what happens when you shut the door to the closet? It gets very, very dark. I also took a kitchen timer into the closet with me and set it for thirty-five minutes while I listened to my tapes because I had the fear that if I fell asleep and my boss opened the closet door looking for me, I'd be fired for sleeping on the job. Ha! I don't think I could have explained to my boss that I was trying to "talk myself healthy."

I share this with you because if you are dedicated to changing the way you think, it will take serious commitment. You have my permission to go inside your closet at work or at home and listen to your positive affirmations, but since today's technology doesn't require us to do such crazy things, it calls to the forefront the choices you make. Will you play music or put on an audiobook instead of listening to positive affirmations or a hypnosis session?

You will get out of this process what you put into it. While you're working to form good habits, make the choice to put your journey to happiness first.

I was married to Don for fifty-four years. We married in the John Wayne era, when wives were treated more like objects. We had many good times. The beginning of the marriage was good; the middle, not so good; the end got better. Let me say this about my marriage: I loved Don very much, but he was an extremely difficult man to live with.

Please understand that I realize our unhappiness was just as much my fault as it was his. And hey, marriage is not easy. No one ever taught me how to be a wife and a mother, or Don to be a husband and a father. This was just "on-the-job" training, and we learned as we lived it! And in all fairness, back then boys were taught to be tough and macho. Boys don't cry. Men are strong and dominating, and if you don't remember the period of the 1940s and 50s, just watch an old Western and see how women were treated. Women were taught to be seen and not heard. This is just the way things were when I was growing up. Thank goodness time has changed this model.

Don always had a lot of self-confidence. When he went into the Air Force in 1962, he was the first *second lieutenant* to ever head up a full squadron at Keesler Air Force Base in Biloxi, Mississippi. He left the Air Force after three years and took a job at a major bank in Baton Rouge in the trust department, then moved into the financial and investments department. When he retired thirty years later, he headed up a small investment cap fund handling two billion dollars in investments.

I thought he was so smart, and because of his background and knowledge of so many financial companies that he invested in, he knew something about everything. Every conversation I'd witness with high-profile investors or just friends, whatever the conversation was, Don knew something about what they were talking about.

The bank had many mergers throughout the thirty years he was there. The last merger moved everyone to Cleveland, Ohio. Don refused to go, and they allowed him to stay in his present job in Baton Rouge. Unfortunately, he was always so negative about everything and was hard on his family and not fun to be around.

We raised two sons, and many times during their childhoods all three of us walked on eggshells. Our youngest son, Brian, could talk to anyone, a one-year-old or a one-hundred-year-old. I told him when he was around fifteen that he should consider a field in marketing, which he did, and he has been very successful in business. Brian had self-confidence and stood up to Don, so Don did not pester him much. Brian liked being around us and did what we expected him to do.

Our other son, Wade, was very likable and enjoyed people. He loved to cook and wanted to be a chef. We called him the Bayou Chef. But he had low self-confidence, and he and his dad would get in constant arguments. Wade never could please him or do anything right. His dad badgered him and put him down in the same way he did me.

I called Wade my wild child. He acted out, was rebellious, and got into drugs and drag racing. I would lie awake every night, waiting for him to come home (usually around 2 a.m.) and finally go back to sleep once I knew he was still alive.

It seemed none of us could do anything right. Don was Dr. Jekyll and Mr. Hyde. But I remembered what my mom told me, and I kept my opinions to myself. This is how things were in our generation. But it still hurt.

I only ever lashed out at him one time. One winter morning I had just fixed myself a cup of hot chocolate. Don and I had an argument about something; I can't even remember what. But he called me "dumb" and "stupid" and wouldn't let up. So I left the kitchen and sat in the living room on the couch, maintaining my calm, using my happiness bubble (more on this later), telling him, "I choose to live in peace and harmony," and would not argue with him, which made him even angrier.

"You're dumb, Linda."

I got up and walked into the bedroom, holding tight to my cup of hot chocolate, trying to find a place to enjoy it in peace. As I sat on the edge of the bed, he walked into the bedroom. I would not look at him. This time he got right in my face, repeating in a loud voice that I was dumb, stupid. He wanted me to feel worthless.

I want you to know that I had never *ever, ever, ever* in my entire life been so mad at another human being. The next thing I knew, I threw the cup of hot chocolate in his face. I can still see his eyes looking at me in shock at what I had done. The hot chocolate was dripping down his face, over his chin, all over his shirt and the bedspread. I realized in horror what I had done.

I did what came naturally and took off running down the hall and out the front door. I walked and cried and walked and cried and walked and cried for over an hour. I didn't know if I needed to run away and never come back or what I should do next. So I prayed to God. "What do You want me to do, Lord?" And somehow, with God's help, I got up the courage to walk back into the house and confront my husband.

I told him, in a loud, commanding voice, "You will never *ever, ever, ever* make me feel that way again."

It was at that moment that I quit trying to fix my husband. I had to work on me. I made a choice. I chose not to be a doormat anymore.

He just stared at me, shocked. I think he realized he had crossed the line and pushed me too far. From then on, he was more careful with his words.

When you stuff down all your feelings, there comes a point when the only way you are going to survive is to learn how to express your deepest feelings to your loved ones in a constructive and positive way. Saying how I felt to my friends, neighbors, coworkers, family members, and especially my husband was just something that I could not do, no matter how angry I was inside. I would harbor hard feelings and resentments for weeks and months on end. I would let him walk all over me.

Around this time, I fell into a deep depression. I don't believe I was ever clinically depressed. I think I was beating myself up with the way I talked to myself (and how my husband spoke to me), and my mind responded accordingly. I fell so far down into my hole of depression that I never thought I would survive. All this was made worse because I hid my true feelings. So, whose fault was that? (Mine.) How could Don or anyone else in my world change their behavior toward me if I never told them that their behavior bothered me in the first place?

When Don and I finally agreed to go to counseling, it was then that I got the courage to tell the counselor that I was unhappy in my marriage. After I explained how I felt, Don looked me straight in the eye with a shocked expression and said, "Linda, I never knew you were unhappy. I am so sorry." So, again, whose fault was that? (Mine.)

Still, my doctor wanted to put me on antidepressants. I was hesitant to take them and told him I was learning about positive self-talk and hoped that one day I may not need the antidepressants.

I considered divorce, and once even told Don so, but he asked if we could try marriage counseling. I truly believe that the biggest problem in marriages today is that people do not communicate their feelings toward each other. How can someone treat you any differently if you do not have the courage to say:

"I feel _____ because _____. What I'd like you to do is _____ ."

I learned this exercise in our counseling sessions. Our homework assignment was to say our "I feel" statements to each other every time one of us made the other mad. Boy, this was not easy for me to do, but I finally, *finally* got good at it, and my life and my marriage started changing for the better.

Later I learned that when you love, like, and respect yourself, you do not let anyone in your life treat you in any way that is different from how you feel about yourself. When you love, like, and respect yourself and stand in your power, people notice that and are attracted to it. They want to be around you because they can feel your positive energy.

If you could ask Don if he considered himself a good husband or father, he would say, "Yes, I provided well financially for my family." Back then it was a man's responsibility to provide for his family, no matter how he treated them behind closed doors. To the outside world we looked like a happy family. It wasn't until the hot chocolate story that my life changed for the better.

I finally realized that I had spent my entire life, and all my energy, trying to please and change this man. The truth was, I had no control over him, and I had to start focusing on me. The only person in my life I had to please was God, and as long as God and I were OK, it did not matter to me anymore what Don or other people thought about me. It took a lot of pressure off me.

Don and me

My inner critic loved to remind me of all the negative things Don said to me about me. That's what your subconscious does. If you stop telling yourself who you are, it will go back to the old thoughts you have about yourself. When I learned to speak over all the criticisms with positive "I am" statements, my life began to turn around.

We have to take control over what we say to ourselves. Our subconscious minds are listening, so we want to only feed it thoughts that will make us better, happier people. Imagine telling yourself every day, "I am intelligent. I am successful. I am good enough."

YOUR BODY IS A TEMPLE

I want you to know that today, I have a very good relationship with God, my higher power. We talk all the time about what's happening in my life—the good and the bad, the lessons I'm here on earth to learn. There was a time, though, when I was on the outs with God.

You see, my relationship with God had a lot to do with my relationship with my dad. Dad and I became a little closer while he was fighting cancer. I took him to his radiation treatments every week, and we would talk some, though not much, as Dad was a quiet man. Dad died six months after his throat cancer diagnosis. At the end Dad went into a coma, but a few days before he died, he came out of his coma and had what is called a rally, which is when the patient all of a sudden seems to be getting better and survival looks possible, but then suddenly, they get worse and then die.

I remember being in the hospital room alone with Dad, and as I was pulling the covers up over his shoulders, he opened his eyes, grabbed my hand, and looked straight into my eyes. "Linda Sue, I love you." Then his eyes closed, and he went back into a coma and never woke up.

My father was only fifty-seven when throat cancer killed him. I was twenty years old and angry that God had not saved my father's life. I grew bitter toward God and stayed that way for years, until I had my first self-hypnosis session with Dr. Winkler.

As Dr. Winkler gave me these wonderful, positive, supportive suggestions—that I was a good and kind person, I was important, I was special, I was loved and could achieve any goal I desired—and as he spoke those words, I could feel God's presence with me. As tears streamed down my cheeks, I let go of all my anger and bitterness toward God.

While I was being hypnotized, I also thought, "What a wonderful job, to be a hypnotist and have the privilege of spending my days giving people these beautiful words of encouragement that I hadn't heard in my own life in a long, long time." When I did decide to become a certified hypnotist, it meant so much to me that both of my hypnosis mentors, Dr. Arthur Winkler and Dr. Paul Durbin, believed as I did in God. In fact, they were both ordained Methodist ministers.

What does this have to do with my body being a temple? I'm getting to that part. Years ago, in 1992, when I had first started my hypnosis practice, I came down with a cold and lost my voice, which is the worst possible thing that can happen to a hypnotist. You can't earn money to pay your bills if you can't talk. Being self-employed, which has a lot of great benefits, unfortunately doesn't give you paid sick days. I actually lost my voice quite often in those days. I canceled a week's worth of new clients waiting to have a session with me.

I remember going to bed one night and having this highly charged conversation with God about having to cancel all my sessions. "I don't understand, God. You are sending me people to teach about self-hypnosis so they can achieve their goals, so why do I keep losing my voice? I can't afford to not work!"

It was at this moment that I heard these words: "My child, the only way we can get your attention is to take your voice away. You need your body here on earth to do our work." Wow! Now, let me be clear, I didn't hear a booming voice; it was just a knowing voice.

I replied, "But God, I am just starting my practice. I have to do everything—be the hypnotist, do all the marketing, clean the bathroom, answer the telephone, purchase all the supplies, etc.!" The knowing voice said, "Ask for what you need, and it will be provided." From that moment forward, all worries and concerns about paying my bills went away because I knew that all my bills would be *paid* by God.

But what was really important to me was that I understood for the first time in my life that I needed to treat my body as a temple. Although I was not overweight, because I was practicing self-hypnosis, which had caused me to stop overeating, I still made unhealthy food choices in my diet. I was still consuming way too many sugars and carbs, and sometimes I would go two months or more before I would eat a green vegetable. Guess what? I thought a potato was a vegetable!

When you care about yourself and take care of yourself, that includes the care of not only your emotional self but also your physical self.

Speaking of caring for yourself, let's get back to the affirmations.

I want to give you two powerful tips to make affirmations more effective. I know you've heard people say, "Oh, I tried affirmations, and they just don't work." Well, maybe they didn't work because the people didn't practice these two critical components.

> **Tip 1: Believe yourself.** When you say the affirmations to yourself, I want you to *feel* them—to act as if they *are true for you*—because remember, your subconscious doesn't care how you want to live your life; it just listens to your thoughts.

> **Tip 2: Close your eyes.** Affirmation recordings are powerful in a normal, awakened state, but when you close your eyes and relax, you allow yourself to experience a natural state of hypnosis. It does something unique to your inner critic, the one who won't stop whispering, "This will never work." Slowly you stop hearing those words because he's gotten bored and moved on to something else. Now that he's out of the way, you are able to let your subconscious really listen to the suggestions you are hearing. This is the moment when you're in the most highly suggestible state of your entire life so that 95 percent of your mind can accept these suggestions as fact.

Are you still not convinced self-affirmations work? Let me tell you a story about Dino Pellissier. His father, Albert, called me several years ago and told me about his ten-year-old son. "Linda, I love Dino, but I do not like him. He is the most miserable child to be around." Then he asked me if I would work with his son.

I agreed, and the first thing I asked his father to do was purchase my *Child's Health and Confidence Positive Affirmation* recording, the same one the kindergarten teacher used during nap time. Albert and his wife, Lisa, made a deal with Dino that every night for fifteen minutes he had to listen to Ms. Linda. They downloaded the recording onto his MP3 player, and he'd pop in his earbuds each night before falling asleep. They'd say goodnight and shut the door.

They didn't know what Dino did once his door was closed. They didn't know if the boy took the earbuds out, but they'd made a deal and were game to wait and see. Every night, they went through this little routine.

Two weeks later Albert and Lisa noticed that Dino was waking up in a better mood. He also wasn't throwing as many temper tantrums. They looked at each other and shrugged. "Couldn't be the affirmation recording, could it?"

They continued having Dino listen, and a week later, after three full weeks of listening to the affirmation recording at bedtime, Dino's teacher, Mrs. Smith, called Albert and wanted to know what he and Lisa were doing differently at home with Dino.

"What do you mean?"

"Something positive is clearly going on with his child. Dino is making better grades. His behavior has really settled down." She further explained how Dino, who is naturally a very shy child, walked up to her that very day and put his hands on his hips. Looking up at her, he said, "Miss Smith, I'm freaking awesome, and you know it, don't you?" She looked down at this little child and thought, "What just happened?"

"So, as soon as I got home tonight, I picked up the phone to call you."

Albert explained the bedtime routine and, after hanging up with Mrs. Smith, couldn't wait to tell me all about Dino's changes.

I hope you're beginning to realize how powerful affirmations are. There is more to Dino's story that I'll share with you in a later chapter. We have more to cover, including the most powerful affirmation in the world.

Are you ready for it?

Day by day, in every way, I am getting better and better than the day before.

If you cannot remember anything that you learned in this book, I want you to remember this affirmation.

───── ～～ ─────

I want to give you a chance to experience the positive affirmation session "Self-Confidence" firsthand, so hit the restroom; then get yourself in a quiet environment, silence your phone, and tell your people you need to be undisturbed for thirty minutes or so.

> **Day by day, in every way, I am getting better and better than the day before.**

The way this works is that I'll make an "I am" statement and then pause. Then you can repeat it aloud or silently back to yourself. But when you repeat it to yourself, I want you to imagine this is really true for you. Remember, this plus closing your eyes makes the affirmation so much more powerful because it helps get your inner critic out of the way. After you've listened, you can continue on with the text below.

"Self-Confidence"

Research has proved that we have somewhere around seventy thousand thoughts a day.[1] And mine used to be all negative. I did not realize what I was doing to myself until I sat in that hypnosis chair and my whole world turned around. Once I realized my mind was listening to my thoughts and trying to make them true, I started worrying about how to take control of my thoughts. Have you ever listened to your thoughts? I wouldn't talk to my dog the way I talked to myself. Do yourself a favor and start listening to how you talk to yourself.

For every positive thought I had, it would be interrupted with a negative thought. It took me years for my inner critic to become my best friend. But I want to share a story about how I started to make some headway. What came next was the most valuable exercise in helping me climb out of that dark hole of depression and not ever fall back in.

AMITE RIVER BRIDGE STORY

In 1993 I had just been recruited from the hospital I was working at to go work for a home health agency in Denham Springs, Louisiana, as their director of human resources. I lived in Baton Rouge and had to cross over the Amite River Bridge every morning going to work, which was about five miles from my home. One day on my ride to work I said to myself, "OK, Linda, you know your mind is listening and responding to your thoughts, so what do you want to think about?"

I made a pact with myself to repeat twelve positive statements that I wanted to bring into my life for the next twenty-eight days. Every time I crossed the Amite River on the way to work, I told myself:

1. I am OK.

2. I am happy.

3. I am important.

4. I am special.

5. God loves me very much.

6. I am having a wonderful day.

7. I am successful.

8. I am confident.

9. I am slim and trim.

10. I am learning to like and love myself more and more each day.

11. I am intelligent.

12. I am getting better and better in every way day by day.

I'd hit that bridge every morning, and in a weak, depressed, low voice I'd squeak out, "I am happy." Then I'd think, "Linda, you don't sound happy." So I'd repeat, "I am happy." Once again, I'd hear my inner critic say, "Linda, you don't sound happy."

So I would force myself to scream the positive affirmations to myself three times in a row in a loud, forceful, chipper voice. "I am happy. I am happy. I AM HAPPY! I am having a wonderful day. I am having a wonderful day, I AM HAVING A WONDERFUL DAY," until I repeated all twelve positive affirmations.

Once I'd get across that bridge, I could feel my endorphins kicking in, and all of a sudden, I felt so good, so alive, and so HAPPY! Then the next day when I crossed the Amite River Bridge, I'd be down in the dumps again, but I was so determined to form this new habit of saying positive affirmations to myself that I just kept it up. Again, I was so used to beating myself up, so I would start screaming again, "I am happy. I am happy. I AM HAPPY!"

I did this for twenty-eight days. People probably thought I was crazy going over that bridge, screaming at myself, but did I care? Nope. I learned how to talk to myself and drown out the noise of my inner critic.

And then the day came when I went to my doctor and asked to be taken off my medication. From that day forward I never felt depressed again, and that was more than thirty years ago.

Like I said, I don't think I had a pathological condition—mine was environmental. I am not telling you to stop taking your anti-depressants. The point here is to use every tool you have available to you, while working with your doctor, so you can learn to talk yourself into a positive mindset.

LIFE-BUILDING STEPPING STONES

In my climb out of the darkness my inner critic threw me into, I discovered some foundational stepping stones that helped keep me on the path to a healthier mindset.

- Stone 1: Have a success plan.
  Your daily affirmation: I will create an achievable plan and stick to it.

- Stone 2: "Fake it till you make it."
  Your daily affirmation: If I believe, I will achieve.

- Stone 3: Take action to achieve your goals.
  Your daily affirmation: I understand that achieving my goal is my responsibility. I will have a plan every day to work toward taking action.

- Stone 4: Adopt healthier habits.
  Your daily affirmation: I love drinking water and eating foods that are good for me.

- Stone 5: Become a smart detective.
  Your daily affirmation: I enjoy adding knowledge of what I learn about my subconscious mind to my daily life.

- Stone 6: Visualize your goal!
  Your daily affirmation: I can see what my life will look like when I achieve my goals.

Marianne Williamson is an author and speaker who talks about the ego and how it can get in the way of our spiritual growth. She famously wrote, "Ego says, 'Once everything falls into place, I'll feel peace.' Spirit says, 'Find your peace, and then everything will fall into place.'"[2]

But I believe we find our peace when we feel comfortable being who God made us to be. Marianne goes on to say, "Our deepest fear is not that we are inadequate. Our deepest fear is that we are powerful beyond measure. It is our light, not our darkness, that most frightens us."[3]

Let this book encourage you to believe these self-affirmations. You are destined to be great! A great parent, a great spouse, a great leader, a great person. Believe what you're capable of, and step into your future.

In the next section we'll be talking about how to direct your mood toward happiness. We'll walk through ways for you to let go of your fears and anxieties. I'll share my story of unspeakable loss and how I managed with Don's deteriorating health. I began to build a spiritual support system around me so I could weather what I knew would be challenging years.

STEP 2 CHAPTER TOOLBOX

What is the biggest takeaway from this chapter? Why?

_____

_____

_____

_____

_____

Look at what you wrote on the "Roadmap to Success" pages in the previous session. Do you see changes in the area you're working on? Record those here.

_____

_____

_____

_____

_____

Start paying attention to how you talk to yourself.

What life-building stepping stones are you ready to adopt today? What is your plan to start including all these in your daily life?

_____

_____

_____

_____

_____

Consider your own "bridge" story, and add to your routine a regular set of affirmations to work on. If you have to, shout them aloud.

_____

_____

_____

_____

_____

_____

_____

_____

_____

Jot some notes here about your self-confidence affirmation session. (How did you feel at the beginning? In the middle? At the end?)

_____

_____

_____

_____

_____

_____

_____

_____

_____

STEP 2
ROADMAP TO SUCCESS

What am I going to do today to be successful in achieving my goal?

1.

_____

_____

_____

2.

_____

_____

_____

3.

_____

_____

_____

4.

_____

_____

_____

5.

_____

_____

_____

6.

_____

_____

_____

7.

_____

_____

_____

8.

_____

_____

_____

9.

_____

_____

_____

10.

_____

_____

_____

Write down any progress you've made on the first goal you set.

_____

_____

_____

Step 3

DIRECT YOUR MOOD TOWARD HAPPINESS

Many years ago my husband and I were at our retirement home on the Gulf Coast when my mother's neighbor called and said, "Your mother is having a heart attack. We called 911, and the ambulance is on the way."

I leaped up and dashed for the phone to call her. After getting the details of what was going on, I said, "Mother, I want you to put your beautiful happiness bubble around you."

MY HAPPINESS BUBBLE

I want to teach you the practice of surrounding yourself in a happiness bubble. This is a practice first introduced to me in the book *Rituals of Healing* by Jeanne Achterberg, PhD; Barbara Dossey, RN, MS, FAAN; and Leslie Kolkmeier, RN, MEd. The practice uses imagery for health and wellness, along with my own interpretations. While they called it the "Protective" Bubble, I changed the name to "Happiness" Bubble to fit better with the purpose of the meditation. I also have an audio version of this meditation available.

Happiness Bubble Meditation

> Get comfortable and close your eyes. Now, in your imagination, let yourself begin to create a beautiful, magical, happiness bubble around yourself. This is your fun, happy, safe place, A place that you can come to anytime you like. Being inside your happiness bubble will help you filter out

thoughts, words, or deeds that you wish to keep out while allowing healthy, positive thoughts, words, or deeds to come into your "sphere" of being.

Your happiness bubble can be any color that you like. Your beautiful bubble is invisible, and only you know where it is around your body and how close it is to you.

Now, I want you to let your beautiful bubble begin to move. Feel it around you as you move the bubble close to your body....Now let it move out away from your skin....Imagine that you wish to protect yourself from an event or a person....In whatever way that feels right for you, become aware of your happiness bubble, and place it wherever you need it to be...close to your skin or farther out from your body....

When you are inside your happiness bubble, you are receiving unconditional love from the Universe. Anyone who has ever loved you, past, present, or future, is sending you unconditional love. Feel it; enjoy it.

All negative thoughts stay outside your bubble. If someone gives you an ugly look or ugly remark, don't worry, it cannot pierce your bubble. It will simply bounce off your bubble into the Universe. If someone wants to argue with you in person or on the telephone, you have permission to say, "I choose to live in peace and harmony," and then physically leave the room or hang up the phone.

This is your special way of protecting yourself, receiving what you wish for yourself, and staying relaxed and calm. Stay here as long as you like, and when you are ready to come back to a fully awake state, all you have to do is open your eyes, feeling safe, loved, and protected knowing you can come here again anytime you like.

Note: Use this exercise in any situation where you feel threatened or out of control. You can imagine extending your happiness bubble like a shield out and around you. You can decide what you wish will enter your bubble (positive statements or people) and what you wish to filter out of it. You can then review the situation later, when you feel relaxed and safe, and objectively evaluate what was said or done.

"Mom, imagine your bubble around you. Just pretend you're in your happy place, and think about how rapidly your body is healing." I closed my eyes and said a prayer for my mom to get to the hospital in time.

When I was in my certification program, each student had to work with fifty clients, record the sessions, and then write up a report to send to their hypnosis mentor. They instructed us not to work with our family members because of the danger that they wouldn't take you seriously.

But when you're getting started, finding people to work with is hard! I asked my mom if I could practice on her. Mother loved hypnosis and was eager to be a guinea pig on every new technique I learned. She even put down smoking her daily pack of cigarettes, a habit she's had for fifty years. As she was riding in the ambulance, headed for the hospital, she knew just how to imagine a happiness bubble surrounding her.

Doctors ran all kinds of tests and discovered that Mother had three blockages, one that they couldn't get to because of its location. They scheduled open-heart surgery. But on the morning of her surgery, she spiked a fever of 103 degrees. They postponed the surgery one day. She kept that high fever for three days in a row while the surgeons waited, continuing to postpone her procedure. Imagine the toll this must have taken on my mom, scared of a serious and risky operation while also fighting a high fever.

At one point her nurses approached me and said, "Linda, after hearing of the danger of the blockages and needing open-heart surgery, your mother should be riddled with fear and anxiety, but of all the patients on our ward, she's the most relaxed. All she wants to do is listen to her cassettes." She was listening to hypnosis sessions on relaxation and positive affirmations.

After Mother's surgery, she went into the intensive care unit to recover. Normally, doctors prescribe patients pain medication—after all, they break your sternum during the surgery. Once again, her nurses approached me. "Your mother doesn't want anything for pain. All she wants to do is listen to her cassettes. We all want to know, What in the world is she listening to?"

This goes to show that a person cannot be both happy and sad at the same time. In the same way, a person can't be relaxed and have pain at the same time. She was putting wonderful healing thoughts into her mind, and it was helping her manage her pain. Hospitals today are using hypnosis more and more to aid in pain management.

<hr/>

So far, we've talked about how powerful beliefs are, how they direct your thoughts, feelings, and actions. If you aren't fully happy in your life, you have to work backward to see what belief might be holding you back. This false belief that you are in some way inferior is your kingpin belief, and it must be removed to find lasting happiness.

We've also discussed the power of "I am" statements and how your subconscious mind listens to your thoughts and tries to make them true. So when your inner critic is shouting that you aren't good enough or smart enough, you have to make statements that silence these lies and convince your subconscious of what is true so your beliefs, thoughts, and actions align with the positive messages.

Now I'll tell you about step 3, learning how to direct your mood toward happiness by calming your fears and anxieties.

THE POWER OF A MENTOR

I'll start by admitting that I strongly believe in mentors and have spent upward of $400,000 in hiring mentors to help me get where I wanted to go. Doesn't it make sense that if you have a goal, you should hire someone who has already achieved that goal—i.e., been there, done that? Someone who has made all the mistakes and can teach you how to get where you want to go faster, smarter, and quicker?

In 1996 I opened the Baton Rouge Hypnosis Clinic. I was what I call a generalist, working with any problem my clients had, not specializing in any one area. I was bringing in around $4,000 a month, enough to pay my bills, but I wasn't making a profit. I decided to specialize in weight loss because I had struggled with an extra forty pounds, and I was determined to develop a hypnosis system for weight loss. I started looking for someone who could mentor me.

Little did I know at that time that God was preparing me for another chapter in my life to unfold because I truly believe that when the student is ready, the teacher shows up.

I had heard about Russell Yarnell, whose clinic consistently achieved one-hundred-pound weight-loss success. He was giving a seminar in Orlando on how to market hypnosis for weight loss. At that time, Russell was mentoring three men in major metropolitan cities. It took me six months to convince him to be my mentor because he did not think this little girl from Baton Rouge could cut it. Well, I am happy to say that I proved him wrong and outperformed the three gentlemen he was mentoring. Two years after opening my business, with Russell as my mentor, I went from $4,000 to $60,000 a month in revenue, specializing in weight loss.

In 1999 I sold my very successful clinic to join Don in retirement. Unfortunately, six months later Don suffered a stroke and could no longer drive. This was a stressful time as we transitioned from being two independent retirees to caregiver and patient. I spent a lot of time in the car, driving my husband to his many appointments. It was a tough time for both of us as we both adjusted to the loss of his independence.

It was made all the more difficult because losing his freedom brought back some old behaviors. He'd slip in comments about me being stupid. In his opinion I couldn't even back out of the driveway the right way to get him to his doctor's appointment. Nothing pleased him. However, two things were about to happen that would put me in the fight of my life.

LOSS

Right after Wade graduated from high school, he and Don had a big fight, which resulted in Wade running away from home. We did not know where he was for over a year. When we finally heard from him, he had married and was attending school to become a minister. We were proud of him.

He and his wife eventually divorced, and years later he remarried, gave up the ministry, and opened his own record shop, selling albums by popular bands. He then divorced again. Six months after he divorced, he moved back home with us.

We let him live with us but said it could be for only three months and that we'd have some conditions, the most important being that he remain drug-free.

Then, after living with us for over *three years*, I discovered Wade was driving Don's car drunk one night while Don was out of town. I was so angry that I told him he needed to find another place to live, or I was going to tell his dad he was driving his car drunk.

Three weeks later Wade told me he had found a place he could rent, a one-bedroom, and he would move out in a week. He went to dinner that night to talk to the friend that said he could live with him.

After having dinner at a Mexican restaurant (with the friend he was going to live with), they left with a light rain on the roads. Wade was in his sports car and, wanting to show off, took a curve too fast and hydroplaned into the path of ongoing traffic.

Wade was killed. The lady driving the other car was headed to the vet; she was also killed, along with their dog. Her daughter was severely hurt but survived. Wade's friend was also severely injured but survived.

I had such severe guilt because I had forced Wade to move out. The husband of the lady driver who was killed also had severe guilt because he was supposed to take the dog to the vet but had wanted to stay home to watch the Saturday football game, so his wife had taken the dog later in the week.

I was numb and in shock and tried desperately to keep busy. I knew well how my mind worked, so I used my positive affirmations, hypnosis sessions, my relaxation signals, and positive self-talk to force myself to feel better. Day by day, in every way, I slowly started to feel better and better. I knew I had a choice. I could be happy or sad, so I controlled what I allowed my conscious mind to think about.

Something the preacher said at Wade's funeral service really helped me. He said when someone dies, we have to realize that person was never ours to keep. God gave us a gift in having that person live with us, and when God was ready to call that person home, that is His prerogative.

I still think about Wade, but now when I imagine him, he's happy. I hope he knows that still today, I would walk a million steps to be able to see him and bring him back.

Don didn't share much about how he coped with losing Wade. Men tend to hold in their feelings. I confessed to Don my guilt over Wade's death, and he confessed he was always too hard on Wade. Saying these things to each other brought us closer.

Years later the strangest thing happened. A few weeks before Don died, he had been in a coma, living at home in a hospice bed. One night Brian had come over to visit, and we were talking, sitting by the side of Don's bed. All of a sudden, Don sat up with a big smile on his face, and looked toward the end of the bed and said, "Hey, Wade," then lay back down and went back into the coma. Brian and I were stunned. I have heard that when people are close to death, loved ones come to greet you to help you transition to the other side. Wow, what an experience!

Don with our two sons, Brian and Wade

A LAWSUIT AND HOW CREATIVE VISUALIZATION SAVED ME

The person who purchased my business had agreed to pay me monthly for five years. One year after the sale—and three weeks after Don had a stroke—the new owner wanted me to buy the business back. He wasn't interested in the daily tasks required to keep the business successful. I wasn't interested in purchasing it back from him. A nasty lawsuit ensued because he refused to pay me the agreed monthly amount.

The lawsuit went to trial, and right before I got on the stand, I started having a panic attack because of all the nasty things his attorney was saying about me to the judge, none of which were true.

I went to the bathroom and tried to calm down. I told myself, "Linda, get a grip." My mind searched for techniques that were sure to calm me down. I took several deep breaths and then started using creative visualization.

Several minutes later, when I emerged from the bathroom and strode into the courtroom, I was in full control, and I claimed the room. I imagined that the room was spun in gold and sparkling, and all my angels were hovering around to protect me. When their attorney started attacking me, I pretended that Wade was there, dressed as a knight in full armor, holding a shield in front of that attorney who kept badgering me and trying to confuse me.

I also used relaxation signals. One of the techniques is the water signal. Every time you see or hear water, you tell yourself you are relaxed and calm, so when I would pause to drink water from my water bottle from the stand, I became more relaxed. The second signal is to rub together your first finger and thumb on your dominant hand, while telling yourself, "I am calm and relaxed. I am self-confident. I am in control."

When the judge asked me a question, I would turn to him, smile, take a sip of water, and respond. Somehow I got through this ordeal, but it was one of the most frightening experiences of my life.

Amazingly, my two attorneys told me later that they had never witnessed someone getting bullied on the stand seem so calm and controlled. "Linda," they said, "it was like you were having a cup of coffee with the judge."

I eventually won the lawsuit.

Two years later, once the noncompete expired, I reopened my business, working out of my home, and have been in business thirty years as of the publication of this book.

My business eventually got so successful that I personally put $100,000 in our personal bank account. I think Don realized, "Maybe she isn't dumb and stupid if she can bring home this amount of money." After that he started treating me more like an equal.

RELAXATION SIGNALS

When working with a client or recording a hypnosis session, I give the client what is called a "post-hypnotic condition response," or a "signal." Anytime the client feels any stress or anxiety, they take a deep, deep breath, exhale slowly, and rub their first finger and thumb together using their dominant hand. They repeat this over and over again, thinking (or saying), "I am calm and relaxed. I am self-confident. I am in control." This signal can be used anytime the client needs help calming down so they feel in control.

I also give my weight-loss clients a signal that anytime they are reaching for food when they are not hungry, they rub their fingers as mentioned and repeat, "I am slim and trim. I am self-confident. I am in control."

Try this next time your desires are weakening your willpower, or when you're upset and can't calm down.

In 2010, in an effort to grow my business and increase my annual income, I invested in conferences and online courses held by some of the most powerful women in my field.

In 2010 I met three of my future mentors when I joined Lisa Sasevich's Sales Authenticity & Success Mastermind Retreat in Arizona at Miraval Spa, which happens to be Oprah's favorite spa: Nikkea B. Devida, creator of MindSonix; Sonia Miller, creator of the Willingness Mantra; and Karin Volo, creator of the Joyometer.

On the first day at Lisa's Mastermind retreat, we were asked to stand up and introduce ourselves. I vividly remember standing up and saying, "My name is Linda Allred, and I am a hypnotist with seventeen years of experience, and I can help people change their bad habits/beliefs in twenty-one to twenty-eight days. I specialize in weight loss, and I just wrote *Weight Off NOW! Get Healthy— Get Happy Self-Hypnosis Home Study System*." I sat down feeling pretty good about myself.

Then, this lady three seats to my left named Nikkea stood up and told the group she had developed a system called MindSonix— and she could change her clients' bad habits/beliefs in two to five minutes, once the highest priority belief was found.

Under my breath I mumbled, "Woman, no way. I don't believe that." But being the curious person that I am, I started checking her out and decided to enroll in her MindSonix Bootcamp online training because I thought, "Would a client rather work with the twenty-one-to-twenty-eight-day lady or the two-to-five-minute lady?' Well, that was a no-brainer. I wanted to help my clients, and if they could get there so much faster than I was showing them, I wanted to explore the possibility of bringing this technique into my Toolbox.

I was so amazed working with Nikkea that I continued my training and became a Certified Expert MindSonix Practitioner, one of only a few in the world. By the way, my clients love Nikkea's program.

Having the support and helpful tools of these women was like spotting a lighthouse while your boat is getting tossed around in a hurricane. And I knew it would bring so much hope to my clients.

Then, in 2011, I enrolled in Karin Volo's three-month online course, Thrive Through Tough Times, and learned about the Joyometer and the importance of being aware of our feelings.

JOYOMETER

Karin introduced us to her Joyometer, a mood management system, and I cannot express how much using Karin's Joyometer daily helped me gain control over my emotions. I printed out my own copy and put it in a special place on my desk. I also put it in a plastic sleeve propped up so I could easily see it.

Karin teaches people how to regularly check in with their feelings and their moods because being aware of them will empower people to choose the feelings that best service them. I set an alarm on my phone to remind me to check in every hour on how I was feeling.

For example, when I started feeling stress, worry, doubts, unworthy, or any other fearful thoughts, instead of staying in those negative feelings, I would look at my Joyometer and ask myself, "Linda, are you in the negative spiral or the positive spiral? You know that you have a choice. You can stay in this dark, fearful, self-pitying mood, or you can move your energy spiral upward toward love, joy, and appreciation. All you have to do is think of something that makes you happy, and you will feel better. Get over yourself!"

Then I would immediately close my eyes and think of when I was in Kauai, Hawaii, looking out over the beautiful turquoise ocean, and I would immediately feel my negative, fearful energy changing from a downward spiral into an upward spiral of positive energy, of happiness, excitement, and hope.

This didn't all happen overnight, as I had formed such a bad habit of always thinking of the glass as half empty instead of half full. But slowly, over time, I used Karin's Joyometer to help me feel better. I am so grateful to this day that I met Karin and that she gifted these tools to the world. I still use my Joyometer today and teach every client I work with how to use it.

Joyometer

For your own copy of the Joyometer, visit Karin's website using the QR code.

Now, when I pray at night, sometimes I'll say, "God, do You remember when I was so unhappy? Do You remember how I would pretend that I was sitting in Your lap and would cry and ask You to put Your arms around me and tell me I was OK? And that You love me very much? God, do You remember when I told You that I hurt so bad that I just couldn't handle these problems anymore, and that I asked You to please take them all away?"

Then I'll say, "God, do You know how truly happy I am today? I am so glad that I am alive. I have found bliss here on earth. God, thank You so much for loving me and helping me understand that I am not alone." Once I understood how self-hypnosis and the laws of the mind worked, I tackled my other problems:

- Overcoming insomnia
- Improving my learning skills
- Beating my emotional eating
- Losing those unwanted forty pounds and keeping them off
- Overcoming my dental phobia

So, let me ask you: What are you hiding from? Are you covering up and stuffing all your feelings by hiding behind those extra pounds, cigarettes, alcohol, or drugs? Whom do you need to tell in your life that their actions are no longer acceptable? What is your life purpose? You do not deserve to be a doormat any longer. If you are unhappy with a situation in your life, tell the person how you feel.

It is up to you to decide how you want your life to look and to take a stand and say, "This doesn't feel good anymore!" And if you are lucky, as I was, the person you love will give you the space to be who you deserve and want to be!

MORE STORM CLOUDS ON THE HORIZON

In March of 2010, just two short months after meeting my three mentors in Arizona, my husband was diagnosed with a very rare cancer. A tumor the size of a football had wrapped around his left kidney. The doctors told us that he had only a 15–20 percent chance of survival. Don underwent surgery, where doctors cut three ribs to remove the tumor. Then, he went through thirty-four rounds of radiation. The cancer went into remission for almost a year. When we learned it was back, it had already spread to his lungs and kidneys.

Don entered what would be three years of the cancer treatment—the last year can only be described as chemo hell. I knew then that Don was not going to live. I began thinking about what was ahead for me after Don was gone, and I knew I wanted the spiritual supportive environment offered through the conferences and online courses.

I really liked Sonia Miller's teachings when I'd met her at the Lisa Sasevich conference in Arizona. Sonia is the author of *The Attraction Distraction: Why the Law of Attraction Isn't Working for You and How to Get Results...Finally*. So when I saw her advertise a yearlong mastermind program called the 90-day Ultimate Manifestation System Intensive (UMSI), I signed up. I ordered her book, which I highly recommend, and read in one of the chapters about willingness. She encouraged readers to come up with their own Willingness Mantra.

DON'T LET FEAR HOLD YOU BACK

When Don was diagnosed with cancer, I had already been in business for almost twenty years, but business was slow. One of my concerns was for the decreased demand of my services. One day I realized the phone had stopped ringing, partially because people knew that I was dealing with Don's illness. But this scared me because I still needed to make a living. What if I had to close the company or file for bankruptcy?

The bills kept coming in, but the clients weren't. Before that time, I never feared not having enough money. I told you the story of how bills came in, and I imagined them stamped "Paid by God" across the front. At that time, money just flowed into the company. But many years had passed since I'd heard that voice assure me. With Don even sicker now, and with little money coming in, all my fears and anxiety flooded over me.

Ever grateful for Sonia's supportive teaching, we spoke about my situation, and she told me that when you let yourself experience fear and anxiety, the universe just collapses down on your thoughts. "Linda, you have to be willing to let your fears and anxieties go." Thankfully, she had a plan to help me turn this around.

Before I tell you how, I want you to think about how many times you've let fear stand between the person you are today and the person you want to be tomorrow. Fear is natural. We all feel it at one point or another, and it isn't always a bad thing. Fear can keep us safe or even inspire us to take positive actions in our lives. Unfortunately, fear becomes a problem when it prevents us from taking steps that would positively impact our future. You may be eliminating future risk, but you're also preventing future reward. For many of us, fear is an obstacle that holds us back from reaching our full potential.

Consider this three-step approach to managing your fear:

1. **Name it.** Instead of sweeping your fear under the rug, put it out there. Write it down, say it out loud, or talk to someone about what's holding you back.

2. **Look at it.** Take a critical look at your fear, and ask yourself why you feel it. Then ask, "What's the worst that can happen?"

3. **Conquer it.** There's only one way to beat your fear, and that's to feel it and do what you've got to do anyway.

THE WILLINGNESS MANTRA

Sonia felt that creating my own Willingness Mantra would help me remember to let my fears and anxiety go. So I drafted what I believed would accomplish that.

When I shared the first version of the mantra with her, she said, "That's good, but we need to add one sentence to make it more powerful." This is the other important element she taught us, and I want to share it with you. I want you to really take this to heart because it can lead you to a lot of opportunities in the future. From this moment forward, anytime you feel any fears or any anxiety, do the following (indulge me here):

MY WILLINGNESS MANTRA

Look up at the sky, or the ceiling of your room—no one will know what you're doing—and acknowledge your fears and anxiety. Say, silently or out loud, "I see you, fear; I see you, anxiety. I honor you and I respect you." Then, take a deep, deep breath, and say, "And I am willing to believe that the universe is going to send me everything I need and want and more in my highest and best good right now, and I am open to receiving from all channels, both expected and unexpected. All is well in my world right now because I know that I am held in the hands of God and I am perfectly and utterly safe. And so I am, and so I am.

I said this Willingness Mantra every day, multiple times a day, during this phase of my life. The one sentence that Sonia wanted me to add to my original mantra was the line about being open to receiving from all channels, both expected and unexpected, because 90 percent of my business at that point came from women, and 10 percent from smart men. "Linda, I want you to put this part in there." She saw the potential before I did.

I want you to know that when I started repeating this to myself, within a week or two, my phone started ringing. Male clients were wanting to work with me. I can remember one man asked me if I accepted cash for a very high-end program working with me privately. Yes sir! And he paid me in one-hundred-dollar bills.

I made more money in a three-week period than I ever made in any three-week period in the previous nine years. This is proof that the universe will send you what you are thinking about!

The universe will send you what you are thinking about!

This mantra is powerful. I had been living in fear and lack. This is one of the main reasons that the law of attraction doesn't work for some people. They stay stuck in their fears and lack. But if you state what you want, believe it, and repeat it, you will get the results you're hoping for, not necessarily in your time frame but in God's perfect timing. So, I want to ask you, What are you willing to believe?

Your goal now is to create your Willingness Mantra and start saying it every day to keep your fear and anxiety at bay. You can write your own, and for help, check out Sonia Miller's book *The Attraction Distraction* for her chapter on

Willingness Mantra

"Willingness." Or you can just use mine, as most of my clients do, and modify it to fit your situation. Pause here and write your Willingness Mantra. Use the blank pages at the end of this chapter if you'd like.

Six weeks before Don died, we brought in hospice. We set up a hospital bed for him in the bedroom with the rails up so he couldn't fall out. He was six feet and had gone from 205 pounds to 140 pounds. He was all skin and bones.

Every night, I would climb over the bed rails and lie next to him, and rub his back. I would play a positive affirmation or a hypnosis CD. One night as we were lying there, he said, "Linda, I never knew I could love someone as much as I love you."

What if I had left the marriage? What if I had walked away?

You see, Don's father never told him he loved him either. He ignored Don as he was growing up too. I think that is why Don liked to put his family down, as it made him feel good, powerful, and in control. And shame on me too, especially because I did not stand up to him when he started in on my boys. We all let him do that to us because we did not have the self-confidence to stand up to him and tell him that his behavior was totally unacceptable.

Some people wait a lifetime to hear those three little words, and some never get to hear them. It didn't fix the challenges we were facing, but hearing those words meant so much to me. Our marriage, like most, was a roller coaster of good times and bad. We had many, many good times. In that moment, I felt happy knowing that after all the years and all those names he called me, here we were, near the end, and what he felt for me was love.

It also reminded me of a story—it's a little crass, but it speaks to the value of going through difficult times with another person. My sister, Janell, and I went to New Orleans years ago to attend Wayne Dyer's three-day motivational conference. On the last day, he said he had a story to tell us that was a little gross but asked if we were up for hearing it. The crowd all cheered and called out, "Yes!"

Wayne said, "I want you to think of the one person in your life that has given you the most grief." Immediately, I thought of my husband. "Now, I want you to close your eyes and imagine that you can see a large white commode sitting in front of you with the toilet seat up. Nod your head if you can see that." We all nodded our heads. "Now I want you to imagine that you can see the biggest, hardest turd that you have ever seen floating in the water in the commode." Well, with my imagination I could even smell it. Wayne then said, "I want you to flush it, and notice that it popped right back up. Now flush it again; it popped right back up. Try one more time—you flush it, but it pops right back up. OK, now everyone, open your eyes.

"I want all of you to know that turd represents your greatest teacher, because if you had not lived with that person, you would not be who you are today."

We all laughed. I drove back to Baton Rouge, and when I walked through the back door and into the den, I could see Don sitting there in his recliner with this cloud of negativity, an ugly smirk on his face because he never liked me going off for the weekend. But I just chuckled to myself, and said, "Oh, there is my turd," and went over to give him a kiss and say hello.

I think of this story so often because if I had not lived with Don and felt all the pain and misery, not feeling good enough, and lack of self-confidence, I would not have become who I am today, able to teach other people like me to learn to like, love, and respect themselves. If you change the way you think, you will change the way you act. If you change the way you act, you will change the way you think.

━━━━∽∿∽━━━━

Our local TV Channel WAFB used to broadcast a health feature every Sunday night with Phil Rainier. Phil showcased me by interviewing my clients, and three of their stories aired on a three-night special. One of the client stories they covered was about a doctor named Dr. Dabney Ewin, a clinical professor of surgery and psychiatry at Tulane University School of Medicine who worked in the burn infirmary in New Orleans. He worked specifically with first-degree-burn victims, which are more serious.

Dr. Ewin suggested that if he could get to the burn victim within four to six hours of the initial burn, he would teach them safe-place imagery, which is another term for hypnosis. He worked with the patients by having them imagine that their body temperatures were cool and they felt no discomfort in their bodies. He told them to imagine their burns were healing rapidly and leaving no scars. His patients healed within three short weeks, with no scarring, whereas most first-degree-burn victims stay in the intensive care unit for six weeks. You knew your mind was powerful, but did you know it was that powerful?[1]

Now I want to tell you about a basketball team that continually lost their games because they could not make their free throws. The basketball coach brought in a sports psychologist who teaches creative visualization, or safe-place imagery, both terms that mean self-hypnosis. He divided the team into three separate groups. The first group practiced the way they always had. The second group got to put in more practice time. The third-group guys could not even go to the gym. For the third group, the sports psychologist had them close their eyes and make believe that they were seeing free throws going through the basket. He asked them to imagine being in an actual game. "What do you see? What do you smell? What do you taste? What do you hear? What do you feel?" The more details, the better.

He asked, "Is it hot? Is it cold? What are you wearing? What colors do you see?" Then he had them pretend they were walking to the free throw line. They shot the basketball and every time, it went through the net. When they brought the three teams back together, which of the three groups do you think made the most free throws? You guessed it, the third group, the ones who couldn't even go to the gym. That is the power of the mind God, or your higher power, gave you.

Many professional athletes use hypnosis, including Tiger Woods and Michael Jordan. Jordan says he "incorporated hypnosis into his training and pre-game routines to enhance his focus and increase his mental stamina."[2]

You don't need pills, drugs, alcohol, cigarettes, or an excess of food. You can achieve your goals using the power of your mind. When you start to experience fear or anxiety, recite your Willingness Mantra. Even if you aren't feeling those negative emotions, saying your mantra every day reminds your subconscious to do all it can to make it true. Remember, the universe will send you what you are thinking about!

I want to share a story I heard years ago at a workshop held in Slidell, Louisiana, by Louis P. Bauer, a certified clinical hypnotherapist. The story illustrates so much of what this book is about. I asked Louis if I could use it, and he granted me permission. Louis and I originally met when I was taking my hypnotist certification with Drs. Arthur and Pam Winkler at St. John's University in Springville, Louisiana.

GEODES HELP US TO UNDERSTAND OTHERS

Geodes were formed millions of years ago. Deep within the earth, water which would normally become steam remained as a liquid because of the tremendous pressure placed upon it and was forced through the cracks, crevices, and cavities within the earth. The extreme heat that is found within the earth dissolved minerals, which then mixed with the liquid until, little by little, the liquid cooled.

The cooler liquid, unable to carry so many sediments in suspension, deposited them in layers inside the hollow spaces within the earth. Sometimes the sediments formed layers, at other times, crystals. Over millions of years, the beautiful interior of the geode developed secretly and silently.

Just as the geode developed in secret, so does the interior life of a person—that part of a person that forms the basis of their personality. Very few ever take the time to look beyond what the eyes perceive and discover the beauty hidden within. As with the geode, a person's outward appearance sometimes disguises that inward treasure.

We are all God's creation. We are made in His image and likeness, we must remember that there is an inner beauty in all of us. Within each of us is a spark of the Divine. As Jesus said, "The kingdom of God is within."[3]

I've told this story of the geodes for years to my clients at the conclusion of our work together. Why? Let's go back to the story of the geodes, and I'll explain.

I ask my clients, "Do you know what a geode looks like?" Most of them say no, so I hand them a solid geode, which looks like a large, ugly, brown, bumpy rock the size of a baseball. I ask them, "If you were on a hike in the mountains, and you saw this rock, would you even bother to pick it up?" Again, most say no. I then tell them how the story of the geode helps us understand others.

You see, when we first meet someone, it takes a few seconds for us to judge if we like the other person or not. We make a quick assessment of how they are dressed and how they talk, and determine if we would like to be around them. For instance, what if you saw a lady who weighed 350 pounds walk into a waiting room where you were sitting? What would your first impression be of her? Most of us (if we're totally honest) may think, "Look at that huge, fat, lazy lady. Boy, how can anyone let themselves become that fat? All she has to do is not eat so much. Oh, please don't come sit by me."

Or what if you saw a drunken man staggering down the side of the road with a sign asking for money? What would be your first impression? "Get away from me. I am not going to give you any money just to go buy more booze. If you need money, get a life and go get a job!"

But if we go back to the story of the geodes, it tells us the geode developed in secret, *as does the interior life of a person—that part of a person that forms the basis of their personality.*" If you really think about it, we don't know what has happened in the past to cause the 350-pound lady to overeat. We don't know what has happened in the past to the man staggering drunk on the side of the road. I have one more metaphor for you to think about. It's about an onion.

I like to describe a person's life using the metaphor of a great big onion—the kind of onion that has that thin yellow covering on the outside and layers and layers of thick onion peel on the inside. Now this is your goal. I want you to strip that onion down layer by layer and get to the smallest part of the onion at the very center. Why? Because that's what these five steps to lasting happiness have all been about—a step-by-step guide to helping you start to strip away all the layers of what I call "walls of hurt and protection" that you have put around yourself since the day you were born.

I truly believe that before we were born, we chose to be put here on earth to learn to love, like, and respect ourselves. And until we learn this, we cannot give love in return because we didn't have it to begin with.

Think about it this way: When you were born, you thought you were pretty special. You loved yourself unconditionally. Hey, you played with your fingers, you played with your toes, your ears, and you even played with your poop! You liked everything about yourself. But one day someone may have told you no, or slapped your hand, and you realized that you couldn't do some of the things you wanted to do.

Maybe they fussed at you and criticized you and made you cry. Maybe you decided that you did not like the way their action made you feel, and you thought, "No one is going to hurt me again. I will put a layer of protection around me," just like the layers of an onion. Then, as you grew older, someone in grammar school or high school made fun of you, and you put on more layers of protection.

Maybe someone called you fat, and you added another layer of protection. Perhaps you were in a bad relationship with someone in college and added yet another layer. Then, you got married and had some pretty rough years, perhaps divorced, and you added a lot more layers of protection around you—until one day you looked at yourself in the mirror, and staring back at you was this great big, yellow onion, surrounded by all these layers of protection so you could never get hurt again.

Let's go back to the story of the geodes. What if you cut the geode rock in half? What would you discover inside? As the story goes, "The cooler liquid, unable to carry so many sediments in suspension, deposited them in layers inside the hollow spaces within the earth. Sometimes the sediments formed layers; at other times, crystals. Over millions of years the beautiful interior of the Geode developed secretly and silently," just as *your* life has developed secretly and silently.

Once it's cut in half, you discover that the inside of a geode is beautiful. The crystals sparkle like diamonds. Now you realize you have probably seen a geode before because the ones you can buy at the store are always cut in half so you can see the dazzling interior. So why am I telling you this?

To help you understand that the goal of the Journey to Lasting Happiness is to help you strip away all the hurts and disappointments that life has handed you; to help you return to the beautiful, sparkling center of your being, just like the geode, where you will discover unconditional love for yourself; to learn to love and like yourself again just as you did when you were a baby; and to understand now and for always that you do not need to use food, drugs, or alcohol as a substitute for love ever again.

When you begin to like, love, and respect yourself, you will discover that you are attracting people to you who really like being around you. Not only do they like you, but they also love you, and they respect you. You would not even think of letting them treat you any other way.

You also understand that God loves the 350-pound overweight lady. God loves the drunken man, and most importantly, you need to understand that God loves *you* very, very much too, and He wants you to be happy. He wants you to learn to love, like, and respect yourself. He wants people in your life to love, like, and respect you as well. You do not need to be anyone's doormat.

Let's keep moving forward. In step 4 we will take a deep dive into hypnosis. Before we shift into that, I want you to recall a few things. The subconscious mind is powerful and is always listening to your thoughts. If you haven't already, stop and really listen to what your thoughts are saying. Is your inner critic cutting you down with criticisms? Repeat the affirmations from step 2! Every day, recite your Willingness Mantra, preferably before you even get out of bed, because the universe is listening. Don't overlook how important this is.

Now tell yourself, "I'm willing to do today what most people won't because tomorrow, tomorrow, I will have what most people won't."

You are well on your way to finding the happiness that seemed to elude you before you began this journey. I am so proud of you for being committed to learning how to reprogram your mind so you can walk through the door of opportunity.

The next chapter is going to be a bit longer than the others because it is the culmination of all we've been working toward. Now, let's get into hypnosis.

STEP 3 CHAPTER TOOLBOX

What is the biggest takeaway from this chapter? Why?

_____

_____

_____

_____

Look at what you wrote on the "Roadmap to Success" pages in the previous session. Do you see changes in the area you're working on? Record those here.

_____

_____

_____

_____

What are you willing to believe about this process?

_____

_____

_____

_____

What are some fears and anxieties you're ready to let go of?

_____

_____

_____

Write your Willingness Mantra, or use mine and modify it as needed.

_____

_____

_____

_____

_____

_____

STEP 3
ROADMAP TO SUCCESS

What am I going to do today to be successful in achieving my goal?

1.

_____

_____

_____

2.

_____

_____

_____

3.

_____

_____

_____

4.

_____

_____

_____

5.

_____

_____

_____

6.

_____

_____

_____

7.

_____

_____

_____

8.

_____

_____

_____

9.

_____

_____

_____

10.

_____

_____

_____

As I make progress toward achieving this first goal, what area do I think I might want to tackle next?

_____

_____

RECOGNIZE SELF-HYPNOSIS IS A LIFETIME TOOL

D ID YOU KNOW that every night, right as you go to sleep, and every morning, right as you wake up, you are in a natural state of hypnosis? What does that mean for you? It means that 95 percent of your mind is listening to your conscious thoughts and doing everything within its power to make your thoughts true for you.

If you are like most people, you take all your problems and worries to bed with you; then you wake up in the middle of the night thinking about all your problems and worries. *Stop thinking this way!* I gained control over thinking about my problems by creating my happiness bubble that I "wore" in the daytime and then made it a sleep bubble at night. Worries or negative thoughts bounced off my bubble back into the universe and left me unaffected.

Hypnosis is sometimes referred to as creative visualization, or safe-place imagery. In a sense it is having a happiness bubble around you so only positive thoughts can enter your mind. When you close your eyes and move the inner critic out of the way, your subconscious can accept what you're seeing, hearing, smelling, tasting, and feeling.

Hypnosis has a reputation in some circles for being nonsense, but it is actually supported and used by many reputable doctors, as we've already discussed. If you feel uncomfortable by the idea of hypnotism mixing with Christianity, I want to tell you a bit more about three very special people who came into my life when I needed them most. I give them credit for shaping my understanding of hypnotism from a Christian perspective.

I met Dr. E. Arthur Winkler, now deceased, and his wife, Dr. Pamela Winkler, in 1990. Art was the founder and president of St. John's University in Springfield, Louisiana, as well as a highly respected author, lecturer, and teacher. He and his wife, Pamela, taught the hypnotist certification program together. Dr. Winkler also wrote many books on the topic of hypnosis and the subconscious mind, including *Mind Medicine: The 40 Most Unusual Cases Out of 40,000 With Hypnosis*. He began using hypnosis in 1962 in his pastoral counseling as a Methodist minister. He went on to hypnotize over thirty-five thousand individuals and helped them overcome their fears and insecurities, excess weight, stress, and smoking addictions, as well as helped them build their self-confidence and self-esteem. Dr. Winkler completed a great deal of research on the subconscious mind that he shares with you in his book titled *Hypnosis: A Key to Health, Happiness, and Success*.

Another person who also had a profound effect on my life is Chaplain Paul G. Durbin, now deceased. He was on the staff at Methodist Hospital from 1976 until his retirement in 2005. He was director of pastoral care from 1982 until his first retirement, in 2001. In 1999 he became director of pastoral care and clinical hypnotherapy. Upon his retirement in 2001 he became director of clinical hypnotherapy and retired again in 2005.

Paul was a retired military chaplain who last served as Army National Guard special assistant to the chief chaplain, with the rank of brigadier general. He took his clinical pastoral education at Walter Reed Hospital in Washington, DC, which was among the first hospitals to offer bedside hypnosis for pain management to their patients. He had his introduction to the value of hypnosis at Walter Reed and began serious training for hypnosis certification in 1981.

I'm happy to say that Chaplain Durbin gave me explicit

permission to use his self-hypnosis scripts, which you will be instructed to listen to later in the book. I invite you to read more about this fascinating individual.

Before Dr. Winkler's death he had also given me permission to use both his positive affirmations and self-hypnosis scripts. My goal, along with Dr. Art and Dr. Pamela Winkler, as well as Chaplain Durbin, is to help people understand how wonderful and special they are and that God loves them very much. Positive affirmations and self-hypnosis help eliminate negative/failure thinking and replace it with positive expectations. Repeat this positive thinking for twenty-one to twenty-eight days, and miracles can occur.

Chaplain Durbin said it best: "The first question most people ask me is, 'Why does a person of religious faith need hypnosis?'" The chaplain's answer reflects his strong faith. "Jesus said, 'I have come that they may have life, and…have it more abundantly.'[1] I believe hypnosis to be a gift of God that helps people experience a more abundant life."

TV personality and cardiothoracic surgeon Dr. Mehmet Oz has spoken many times about the benefits of hypnosis for helping with lifestyle changes such as smoking cessation, pain management, or weight loss. Dr. Oz is careful to note that participating in hypnosis should be part of a comprehensive approach to wellness, alongside medical and lifestyle professionals.

Clinical psychologist Dr. Michael Yapko is a well-respected doctor and expert in hypnosis. His books *Trancework: An Introduction to the Practice of Clinical Hypnosis* and *Hypnosis and Treating Depression* have helped millions. Dr. Yapko has done extensive research on how hypnosis can aid in treating depression and anxiety.

Hypnosis isn't only embraced by clinical hypnotherapists. Many other professional fields practice hypnosis for the positive effects it offers patients. Psychologists and therapists practice hypnosis with patients who have conditions such as anxiety or trauma. As I've already shared, professional organizations such as sporting leagues have incorporated visual imagining to help athletes mentally prepare for a competition. I've shared a few examples of how, in the field of medicine, doctors have used hypnosis to help burn victims and those suffering with chronic pain. Perceiving hypnosis as a form of quack medicine is simply an outdated and uninformed assessment. Dr. Winkler said,

> Every day more people are learning the many advantages to be gained through the use of self-hypnosis. The idea that hypnosis is some kind of supernatural power or ritualistic magic is being replaced with true, scientific facts that are helping people realize hypnosis is a tool that can be used by all intelligent people to help themselves in numerous ways. People are finally developing confidence in hypnosis—a confidence that has been established as the result of years of experiments and research in the field of physical and metaphysical science.

"What the Heck Is Self-Hypnosis?"

Having outlined legitimate uses of hypnotherapy, I would be remiss to not mention the importance of working with a qualified professional who is properly trained and certified so you get the results you want.

HYPNOSIS 101

Understanding the laws of the mind is a life-changing concept. Your subconscious mind keeps your heart pumping the blood through your circulatory system, keeps you breathing, enables your digestive system to continue functioning properly, enables you to talk when you decide to talk and walk when you decide to walk, and has been doing thousands of other things that your conscious mind has *not* been consciously aware of. The importance of all this is realizing that you can trust your own subconscious mind to take care of you.

We talked about this in step 1, but it is worth repeating. Your conscious mind is called your left brain, your critical faculty. It judges and analyzes everything you do. This is where your inner critic lives. On the other hand, your subconscious mind does not judge; it is literal. It believes anything you tell it. It is like a computer. Whatever you tell it to do, it does.

I'd like to share some very valuable information I learned from a seminar I attended:

- When you are six years old, 60 percent of the belief of who you are has already been formed.

- When you are eight years old, 80 percent of the belief of who you are has already been formed.

- When you are fourteen years old, 99 percent of the belief of who you are has already been formed.

But you can begin to change your thoughts. Remember that in step 1 we talked about neuroplasticity? Your brain is not locked in an unchanging, permanent state. New ways of thinking form new pathways, and new habits can form and stick. You're never too old to change a habit! I'm living proof of that. Again, if you think a thought, whether positive or negative, for twenty-eight days, it forms a habit in your subconscious mind and becomes what you really think and believe about yourself. Simply put, your thoughts become a self-fulfilling prophecy. This is why "stinkin' thinkin'" is actually so risky to your well-being. If you want to be happy, don't give your inner critic any room to live in your mind.

You are actually bringing into your life what you are thinking about, not realizing that you are asking for and receiving the exact opposite of what you want. Some people call this the laws of attraction, and the book *The Secret* helped drive home the same point I'm making here. (By the way, one of my mentors, Loral Langmeier, was featured in *The Secret*. She teaches you how to become a millionaire.)

Even those thoughts you have in secret come to pass. You do not have to say the thought out loud, and whether you believe the thought or not does not matter; your subconscious mind will try and try again to make your thoughts come true. That is why you need to learn to approach your goal as though you have already achieved it.

HELPER, RESISTOR, KING/QUEEN FOR A DAY

You understand that you can lose weight by simply zipping your mouth shut and starving yourself to death. But what happens when you unzip your mouth and go back to your old bad habits? You gain back the weight you lost, plus more! Your journey to finding lasting happiness is a lifestyle, behavior modification, *and* self-hypnosis system.

Let's do a quick check-in now to see how sold you are in believing self-hypnosis will work for you. On a scale of 1 to 10, with 10 being the highest, rate if you firmly believe that not only are you going to learn how to achieve the goal you want, but more importantly, you are going to also use self-hypnosis to learn to maintain your new habits moving forward.

There are no right or wrong answers here. I'm just taking your temperature to see where you are at this moment as well as helping you understand how important strong beliefs are.

Helper

There are three ways to experience hypnosis. The first way is what's called a helper. Let's say I have you in the state of self-hypnosis and suggest that your eyes feel so heavy that you cannot open them. A helper might sit there, thinking, "My eyes do not feel heavy. Oh, my goodness, what am I going to do? This crazy woman wants my eyes to feel heavy, and they don't. Well, if I'm going to lose this weight, then I'm going to pretend that my eyes feel so heavy I cannot open them."

Let me tell you something. Not to sound harsh, but I don't need help from you. You understand you have been trying to help yourself for years, and it hasn't worked, right? If your eyes do not feel heavy, and you can open them, then open them. The reason your eyes aren't heavy is that some people are very visual; they can see things in their mind. Some people are auditory; they just like to hear things. And some people are kinesthetic; they prefer to feel things.

If you open your eyes when I give you the suggestion that you can't open them, it does not mean you weren't hypnotized. It just means that you respond better to another type of suggestion, which is why the recordings are designed to assess all your three types of learning: visual, auditory, and kinesthetic.

Resistor

The second way to experience self-hypnosis is as what's called a resistor. This one never ceases to amaze me. I don't know why people pay me a fee, sit in my chair, then lean way back with their hands folded across their chest, looking at me belligerently, as if saying, "Go ahead! See if you can hypnotize me! I don't think you can, but go ahead and try." It doesn't make any sense to pay me and then resist my suggestions. You do want to achieve your goals, don't you?

King/Queen for a Day

The third way to experience hypnosis is as a king/queen for a day, and this is the disposition I'd like you to have. What if you won a fabulous vacation to a five-star resort? You can go anywhere in the world—the French Riviera beaches, the Swiss Alps, Niagara Falls, Mount Everest. As you are sitting in your recliner, feeling as if you are a king/queen for a day, you also have five people at your beck and call. Does that sound like an experience you'd be interested in? That's how I want you to experience your self-hypnosis sessions. Just sit back and enjoy the experience, and let me do all the work.

WHAT HYPNOSIS IS AND ISN'T

My goal is to help you understand what self-hypnosis is and isn't. Have you ever daydreamed? That is self-hypnosis. What about aimlessly staring at a candle or a fire roaring in a fireplace? You're feeling relaxed and focusing on the flame, but you hear the sounds of what's going on around you. Yet if someone asks you a question, you may not hear them because your focus is on something else. That's a natural state of self-hypnosis.

Have you ever been watching TV or reading a book, and someone asks you a question and you did not hear them? That is self-hypnosis. By the way, television is the biggest hypnosis market in the world. Why? All the advertisers are constantly giving you suggestions for buying their products—if you've ever bought something you saw on a TV commercial, that is proof of the power of suggestion!

My favorite way to experience self-hypnosis is through what is called road hypnosis. I'll be riding down the road and pass right by my turn. Has that ever happened to you? Or you've driven to work on autopilot and have parked your car and thought, "I don't even remember taking the exit to get here." These are all natural states of self-hypnosis.

Understand that every human being alive goes into a natural state of hypnosis at least four or five times every day. If I could sit on your shoulder during your day and wait for you to naturally go into a state of self-hypnosis, I'd immediately give your subconscious mind some new beliefs. For example, if you were trying to lose weight and if sugar or chocolate was a problem for you, I would tell you, "Sweets and chocolates no longer have the same seductive appeal they once had—they are not good; they are not bad; they just are not important anymore," and you would accept these suggestions immediately. Why? The power of suggestion.

What if you're trying to stop smoking? Again, if I could sit on your shoulder, I'd tell you, "You are a nonsmoker; you are self-confident; you are in control," and you would accept the suggestions immediately. You can thank the power of suggestion.

What if you're hoping to break free from excessive stress? I'd give you the suggestion, "You are calm and relaxed; you are self-confident; you are in control." You would accept these suggestions immediately because of the power of suggestion.

But the problem is you are going to get one heck of a backache if you have to carry me around all day long on your shoulders as I wait for you to naturally go into a state of self-hypnosis so I can give you positive suggestions. So, what I suggest you do is sit in one of your comfortable recliners in the privacy of your own home, click the link to play the recording, and let your conscious mind—your inner critic—go off on its own. It doesn't take but a few minutes for your conscious mind to get bored, get out of the way, and make room for your subconscious mind to readily accept the new suggestions.

There is a difference between using positive affirmations and self-hypnotism. In the positive-affirmation sessions, the person keeps their eyes open. If the person closes their eyes, it makes the session much more powerful because our imaginations are freer. When you close your eyes in the first minute or so, and keep them closed, this is when it becomes self-hypnosis.

Some other common questions I get asked are:

What if I can't be hypnotized?

In all my years of hypnotizing thousands of people, I've seen very few people not able to enter into the necessary state of relaxation that allows self-hypnosis to work. As long as you can hear the positive suggestions being spoken, hypnosis will work. However, if you are drunk or on drugs that cause changes in behavior and perception, or if you are mentally impaired, hypnosis may not be effective because you will not be able to hear and take in the positive suggestions given.

This brings up another point. Some will say afterward, "I don't think I was hypnotized; I heard every word you said." Yes, that's the point! You will hear my voice.

Can self-hypnosis work for me?

If you have an open mind and are willing to give your hypnotist 100 percent of your commitment and cooperation, then she/he will do the rest. I'm positive you'll be excited about the results from your sessions.

Will I be asleep through the process?

First off, self-hypnosis is not a sleep-inducing treatment. Forget what you've seen on television about hypnotists swinging watches and making people act silly on stage. You cannot be made to say or do anything that you don't want to do—it's that's simple. You're in charge of the session and can stop anytime you want.

That's enough talk *about* hypnosis; let's give you your own experience.

HYPNOSIS SESSION

Let me ask you a question before we proceed. If you could prove to yourself that your mind responds to your thoughts, whether those thoughts were good or bad, would you be more open to learning how self-hypnosis can help you achieve your weight-loss goals?

Hopefully you answered a resounding "Yes!" because this is the main belief you need in place in order to achieve the most from self-hypnosis training.

Now, I'd like you to experience a self-hypnosis session. This is one of my favorites, a session called Ultimate Relaxation. Who doesn't want to feel that? This is sure to compete with some of the best massages you've had over the years.

A bit of background on this session. I created the Ultimate Relaxation hypnosis session after I met Jan, one of my clients, at a Make Today Count cancer support meeting. I got involved with this organization early in my career because after my dad died from throat cancer, I was determined to use my skills as a hypnotist to help reduce the stress of cancer patients.

When I walked into the meeting, Jan was crying hysterically and the group was trying to comfort her. Jan said she had bladder cancer and the cancer had gone into remission, but now, six months later, it was back. At her first chemo treatment, they had to tie her down to keep her from falling out of the chair because she was shaking so badly from fear.

Jan enrolled in my Stress Management Program, and on her

second visit I did a guided imagery hypnosis session where she pretended she was walking down ten flights of stairs, relaxing more and more with each step down. She then entered a cottage and sat in a recliner. I asked her to imagine she felt total peace and a healing light from above was shining on her.

At the next meeting, Jan reported that at her next chemo visit, they did not have to tie her down, as she was more relaxed, but she was still scared. She said, "Linda, would you please tape this session for me? I know if I had your voice in my head, I could get through this more easily."

I told Jan I didn't even own a tape recorder, but I would see what I could do. So I borrowed an old tape recorder from a friend and recorded the session for her on a cassette. (Do you remember cassettes?) Jan came in the week after I gave her the recording, hugged me, and said, "Linda, I got so relaxed and calm listening to your voice during my chemo treatment. I actually pretended in my mind that I was in a beautiful place in the piney woods where I live. I also imagined that I was swinging on a hammock in Hawaii. It was wonderful. Thank you so much for doing this for me."

It was at that point in my career I realized how powerful it was to give my clients a copy of their session as a reinforcement tool to use at home. On May 20, 1994, our local newspaper, *The Advocate*, did a full-page story about Jan in the "People" section.

Please note that even if you fall asleep and hear nothing that you are being told on your recording, you will still benefit because the subconscious mind hears everything, even if you are asleep. However, you will benefit more if both your conscious and subconscious mind hears the suggestions that you are being given on the recording.

"Ultimate Relaxation"

Now, are you tired of reading all about hypnosis and ready to *do* it? Let's go. Click on the QR code.

HOW CAN LEARNING SELF-HYPNOSIS HELP ME?

Practicing self-hypnosis regularly is a natural stress releaser. All you have to do is sit in a comfortable chair or lie on your bed and give your mind and body permission to slow down. You do this by learning to take some deep, deep breaths while listening to your self-hypnosis MP3s. Your body, mind, and spirit will thank you for this wonderful, quiet, and relaxing time.

Understand that nothing in your life will change; you will still have your same stressors, but when you practice self-hypnosis and learn to let go of your stress in a healthy, natural way, things in your life sort of naturally slow down. You will notice that you will be able to handle your daily problems better, you will become a lot calmer and more relaxed, you will sleep better, you will have more self-confidence and self-esteem, and your memory will even have an opportunity to improve because when you slow down, your mind becomes clearer.

Who can remember things when their minds are so cluttered and foggy from constantly running on the treadmill of life? You are going to learn to get high on self-hypnosis! You read that right. It is legal, it is free, and you can do it anywhere except while driving a car.

Self-hypnosis is the quickest and easiest way to jump-start your desire to change your bad habits—no drugs, no long treatment plans, no ongoing costs.

An *American Health Magazine* study shows how effective hypnosis is compared with other methods:

- Psychoanalysis: 38 percent (after six hundred sessions)
- Behavior Therapy: 72 percent (after twenty-two sessions)
- Hypnotherapy: 93 percent (after six sessions)[2]

In most cases you'll see results much faster than with other programs. But please understand, once you have jump-started your new behavior patterns, it is still *your* responsibility to keep working these five steps. You have to engage your conscious mind as well as your subconscious mind. It's all about follow-through.

Your subconscious mind wants to go back to the old behavior. Don't believe me? Move one of your trash cans at work or home to the opposite side of your desk, and see how many times you throw the trash on the floor. This is why I asked you to write down your commitment and even sign a Responsibility Contract. Change is hard!

I'd like to share a testimony I received that shows one person's experience of hypnosis after behavioral therapy wasn't effective.

Working with Miss Linda has truly been a transformative force in my life! When I found myself in the throes of a toxic relationship, struggling with severe depression and anxiety, I was desperate for a way out. The COVID-19 pandemic brought unexpected changes, including a new work-from-home job, which only amplified the negative dynamics in my relationship and ultimately led to the end of my engagement.

Feeling lost and unsure of how to reclaim my identity, I turned to hypnosis as a potential solution. During this search I discovered Miss Linda online, and from our first session, I knew I was in good hands. Despite already under-going cognitive behavioral therapy, I felt as if I was spiraling downward rapidly. I felt overburdened, trying to juggle the needs of my daughter, my work obligations, and the isolation the lockdown imposed.

Miss Linda's approach to hypnosis was truly remarkable. She helped reset my negative thought patterns and equipped me with practical tools to regain strength and rediscover who I truly am. During our sessions, she mentioned that she had never witnessed such profound shifts within a client, both mentally and physically, which left me physically drained but mentally prepared to embrace positive change.

Thanks to Miss Linda's guidance, I've experienced a remarkable transformation. I've cultivated new, positive rela-tionships and landed my dream job—an opportunity I never thought possible. Working in a clinical role, advocating for individuals with intellectual and developmental disabilities is not just a job; it's a deeply meaningful pursuit that aligns with my values and aspirations.

Although I'm sad about Miss Linda's retirement, her influence on my life is immeasurable. Together we delved into various aspects of my life, addressing issues and unlocking potential that have empowered me to pursue my dreams with renewed vigor. Miss Linda's influence has strengthened my outlook on life and made me a more resilient and self-assured individual.

I want to express my deepest gratitude for her unwavering support, guidance, and transformative influence. She has helped me find my voice again and has paved the way for a brighter, more fulfilling future.

Thank you, Miss Linda—I am forever grateful!

—SANDRA TRAMMELL, RN, BSN, CCRN

Look at it this way: You can pay the best golf pro in the world to teach you and give you lessons on how to play a better game of golf, and week by week, month by month, your game of golf will improve. But if you quit practicing what you learned, your newfound knowledge is going to fade away, and you'll quickly find yourself right back where you started—being an unsuccessful golfer. On the other hand, if you continue practicing what the pro has taught you, every day for the rest of your life, you will soon be a great golfer. The same is true if you practice your new behaviors for the rest of your life. The more you apply yourself, the better and longer lasting the results will be.

Years ago a client came to me after having just seen her oncologist, Dr. Jay Brooks with the Ochsner Clinic in Baton Rouge, Louisiana. Dr. Brooks had told her to put her affairs in order, as her brain tumor had grown and there was nothing more they could do. She had only a few months to live. I told her that I could teach her some stress-management techniques as well as creative visualization. She enrolled in my Stress Management Program.

I asked her if she could imagine her brain tumor shrinking. She said yes, that her father was a carpenter and she could imagine him chipping away at her tumor.

"I want you to intentionally, every time you can, sit down and close your eyes and imagine this scenario. Especially do it every night and every morning when you awaken." So she imagined the tumor being chipped away like a wooden block.

The most amazing thing happened. The tumor shrunk. Dr. Brooks could not explain it, and all I could say was the mind is powerful. She lived three more years. When I went to her funeral, her husband hugged me tight and told me that the greatest gift his wife received was learning to feel in control of her life. He thanked me for giving her that gift.

Before we move on to the final step, I want to tell you about losing Don. No amount of hypnosis or creative visualization was going to save him from the cancer that eventually took his life. I don't share these personal stories to shine a spotlight on myself but to show you that no matter what comes at you in this life, you can get through it.

CHEMO HELL STORY

Don and I had some really good years and enjoyed being together.

Then one day he finally confessed to me that he was not feeling well and needed to make a doctor's appointment. I knew that it had to be something serious because Don was terrified of doctors and had what they call white coat syndrome. This was a fear caused as a young boy growing up, seeing his mother almost die from seven or eight major surgeries.

When the doctor examined Don, she felt a large lump on his left side and scheduled an MRI immediately. The results were terrifying, as they revealed a large tumor, and the prognosis was cancer.

I remember going to a coffee shop to have a cup of coffee after we left the doctor's office, and Don's hands were shaking so badly he could hardly keep the coffee from spilling out of the cup. We both looked into each other's eyes, knowing that our life had changed instantly for the worse.

Surgery was planned in three weeks, but a week before, when I had gotten home from shopping, I found Don sitting in his office chair with the sandwich I had left him still uneaten, and in a semicoma. I immediately called the doctor. She said to call 911, and they took Don to the hospital in an ambulance.

The surgery revealed a large mass completely wrapped around his left kidney—so large, in fact, they had to completely remove the kidney and cut out two or three ribs to get the large mass out. The doctor said the tumor was the size of a small football. The doctors also said they did not think he would survive the night. I remember my son Brian and I sat on the floor all night in the waiting room, knowing that any minute they would come tell us Don had died. Surprisingly, though, he survived.

We then spent five weeks in the hospital, with me sleeping on the hard, plastic couch the hospital provided for the spouse. Three weeks in I told Don that I could not sleep there anymore and that I would be there at 7:30 a.m., stay with him all day, but wanted to go home at 6 p.m. The nurses come in every thirty-plus minutes, checking on him throughout the night, so no one could sleep. We were both exhausted.

We finally went home; then, five days later, we were back in the hospital again, to the hard hospital plastic couch. The good news was when the oncologist came in, he said the cancer was contained within the kidney and we did not have anything to worry about. On our follow-up visit, we discovered he'd been wrong. The cancer was wrapped around the outside of the kidney, and the cancer was not contained.

Don's plan of treatment was radiation. Don did OK with the thirty-four radiation treatments, only having a few discomforts along the way. However, six months later the cancer reared its ugly head, showing up in his lungs and liver.

The doctor then suggested chemo, and our year of chemo hell began. I was the bold one and asked about the survival rate of this cancer, small tissue sarcoma. The doctor said Don had a 15–20 percent chance of survival, as it was a rare cancer and there were not many treatments available. Not the words we wanted to hear.

Don did not do well with chemo. In fact, his very first chemo treatment put us back into the hospital. When I saw that small, crowded room they had put us in, and especially that hard, plastic hospital couch, I totally lost it. I told the nurse that this room was totally unacceptable. Don looked at me and said, "What is the matter with you, Linda?" I burst into tears. What was the matter with me? I just wanted things to get back to normal. Just normal.

I remember a networking friend had said to me, "Linda, this is going to sound harsh, but listen to me. My husband died of kidney cancer. It is a long, long-drawn-out affair. There will come a day when you wish your husband was dead so that things will be normal again. Linda, when that happens to you, you are not a bad person to think this way. We are only human."

I had been Don's full-time caregiver up until this point. One especially bad day I called my sister, Janell, and broke down in tears. I told her that I was totally exhausted and I was deeply, deeply depressed. She said, "Linda, who do you think you are, Superwoman? You are taking care of Don while at the same time trying to keep your company afloat. Call your doctor tomorrow, or I am going to fly down from Norfolk, Virginia, and take you there myself.

When I went to the doctor, she gave me a questionnaire to see how depressed I was. Well, guys, I failed the test miserably. I realized Janell was right, so I hired Rose, a wonderful, loving, supportive nurse aide to help me during the day, along with a night nurse to help at night with Don.

I then moved into the spare bedroom next to Don, with a baby walkie-talkie next to me so I could hear everything the nurse said to Don and to make sure he was OK. From then on, I visited Don when I wanted to, like a friend, and left when I wanted to, and the nurses took care of his physical needs.

I can tell you that it is hard to just let go and let someone else take care of the one you love. I can tell you that it is hard to watch someone you love go from a handsome, healthy six-foot-tall man to a gray-mass skeleton of 140 pounds and wither up and die right in front of your eyes.

So why did I tell you this chemo-hell story? Because if this happens to you, or a loved one, I want you to realize that you have learned many, many relaxation techniques that can help you or help someone you know.

I had my Roadmap to Success sheet with me at all times because I had written down all the things that I knew could help me get through this. Here is a list of the techniques I used:[3]

- I lived in my Happiness Bubble. I refused to accept negative thoughts and tried to keep my mind positive. Did I succeed all the time? No, but it worked a lot of the time.

- I would scream positive affirmations out loud as often as I could.

- Day by day, in every way, I am getting better and better than the day before!

- I listened to my MP3s: Positive Affirmations: Reduce Anxieties, Self-Confidence, Healthy Living, Improve Sleep, Self-Hypnosis, Ultimate Relaxation, Greatest Secret

- I used my Willingness Mantra

- I used my Joyometer

The moral of my story is if I can get through this, I can get through anything—and so can you!

Two or three weeks before Don slipped into a semicoma, he was still strong enough to walk to the bathroom with Rose's help. One day Rose came running into the kitchen to tell me she could not get Don off the commode. We both tried to lift him, but his weak legs just did not have enough strength for him to stand up.

After numerous tries we finally lifted him, but he fell to the floor right outside of the bathroom. Again, we tried to lift him but failed. Over and over again. I told him I needed to call 911 to help us. I will never forget his eyes, penetrating into mine, with the raw look of a formerly strong man, now broken, who was once so alive and who now could not get up. He pleaded with me not to call 911. So I didn't.

Rose and I looked at each other and said, "OK." I went and got Don's wheelchair to try to lift Don into it. Rose grabbed his legs, and I took the heaviest part of him, putting my arms under his arms, and tried to lift him. I cannot recall exactly how many tries it took for us to get this man into the wheelchair, but somehow we did it. We wheeled him over to the bed and managed to get him situated back under the covers. From then on, we decided to use a bedpan with him, another horrible moment for Don to face.

Let me say this: Don was the most wonderful patient anyone could ever ask for. He never complained. He could have made the end of his life so much worse for me by complaining about all the horrible chemo reactions he was having. But he didn't. I will always be grateful and love him more for how well he responded to events he could not control.

The day Don passed, I had gone to a pain-management specialist, as I had pulled my back out when Rose and I lifted Don into his wheelchair. His twenty-four-hour nurse was there when I walked into the back door. She looked at me and said, "Linda, Don passed about an hour ago." In the shock of hearing those words, my first thought was this: "What a gift," because I knew Don would not want to pass with me at his side.

I ran into the bedroom, climbed over the hospice bed rails, and lay on top of him, sobbing. I instantly felt how cold Don was. I will never forget the feeling of his body, blood no longer pumping to keep him warm.

Even though I knew from the beginning, when the doctor told

Don, he had only a 15–20 percent chance of living, and that eventually I would lose him, even three years later, knowing this, you are never, never, ever, ever ready to lose the person you love.

I lay on his body for over an hour, wailing like an animal who had been shot. The nurse called my neighbor Colleen—who died two years ago with multiple myeloma cancer—to come over and comfort me, and I will always be grateful to her. Then, somehow, numb and stumbling, I called my son Brian and told him his father had just passed. Then the planning of the funeral began, and life got busy again.

Cancer is such a horrible disease, and hopefully one day there will be an easy, pain-free way to prevent or cure cancer. I know I will smile when that day comes.

After Don died, I continued to say the Willingness Mantra, sometimes fifty-nine times a minute. I would crawl in bed and pull the covers up over my head. I just wanted the whole world to go away. Thirteen years as a caregiver, and I was so beat down, physically, mentally, emotionally, and spiritually. First, he had a stroke and couldn't drive for six and a half years. Then, a couple of years later, he developed cancer. It was the end of a three-year battle when he finally passed. Some days I felt as though I couldn't get up and take one more step. I was down in this hole of grief.

At the same time, I also knew how my mind worked. As I lay there, I thought, "Linda, you can stay here and have another pity party, or you can get up and choose to be happy. You're getting back exactly what you're thinking about." So I'd get motivated and throw the covers off and stand up, tears streaming down my face, and head to the kitchen to make myself a cup of hot tea.

As I fumbled around the kitchen, I'd tell myself, screaming in a loud voice, "I am happy! I am having a wonderful day! Day by day, in every way, I'm getting better and better than the day before!" By the time I'd made my cup of tea, the tears would have stopped, and I'd be OK until I crawled back into bed that night and start the whole cycle over again.

I did not let my fears and anxieties collapse on me. I was in complete control of how I felt and how I would live my life. You become what you think. I had to keep doing this exercise over and over again, training my inner critic to be my best friend. I said the Willingness Mantra so much I started to believe myself.

Six months after Don died, I pulled a legal envelope out of the box to mail something and came across one that said, "Linda, I love you," written on the blank envelope. It was like a message sent to me from heaven. He knew I would eventually discover it. After struggling a lifetime to say these words, they were the final words he left me.

That story was hard to write, so I know it was hard to read. But please know those dark days of grief did not last forever. Happier times are coming!

Can you believe it? We're moving on to the last step! You've done such great work, and I'm proud of your commitment to change your lifestyle so you can be happier. The final step will cover the importance of beating your bad habits and will give specific suggestions for overcoming the weak areas from your Wheel of Life—and I threw in a few extra gifts for you. Hang on; we're getting close to the end!

STEP 4 CHAPTER TOOLBOX

What is the biggest takeaway from this chapter? Why?

_____

_____

_____

Look at what you wrote on the "Roadmap to Success" pages in the previous session. Do you see changes in the area you're working on? Record those here.

_____

_____

_____

_____

Have you ever daydreamed? (You heard every word someone said, but you did not answer, or you missed your turn while driving? That is self-hypnosis.)

_____

_____

_____

Before the hypnosis session, would you have considered yourself a helper, resistor, or king/queen for a day?

_____

_____

_____

Did you hear every word that I said during your first self-hypnosis session, "Ultimate Relaxation"? Did you notice that you felt the suggestions I was giving you?

_____

_____

_____

Jot down some thoughts you have on the relaxation hypnosis session.

_____

_____

_____

_____

_____

Has your perspective changed about how you view hypnosis, now that you've gotten firsthand experience? How was the session different from what you imagined?

_____

_____

_____

Will you replay this session in the future?

_____

_____

_____

_____

STEP 4
ROADMAP TO SUCCESS

What am I going to do today to be successful in achieving my goal?

1.

_____

_____

_____

2.

_____

_____

_____

3.

_____

_____

_____

4.

_____

_____

_____

5.

_____

_____

_____

6.

_____

_____

_____

7.

_____

_____

_____

8.

_____

_____

_____

9.

_____

_____

_____

10.

_____

_____

_____

As I make progress toward achieving this first goal, what area do I think I might want to tackle next?

_____

_____

What will be the next goal I work on?

_____

_____

_____

STEP 5

GET THE RESULTS YOU WANT

I N 2014 I hired Nick Nanton and his Celebrity Branding Agency out of Orlando, Florida, to brand me as a Mindset Mastery expert. The success of that partnership led to my first best-selling book, coauthored with Lisa Sasevich, titled *Answering the Call*. In 2014, eighteen months after Don passed away, I won a Quilly Award for that title.

My branding also resulted in the Woman's Prosperity Network (WPN) choosing to sell a course based on the material in this book. I was on their teaching faculty for four years, and they marketed my course to their worldwide community.

I was a contributor in Women's Prosperity Network's best-selling book *Journey to the Stage*, where I wrote about how I became the hottest ticket in town at the young age of seventy-four. I hired Loral Langmeier in 2015 and traveled around the country and Canada with her Live Out Loud community for the Three Days to Cash workshop, teaching how to help people become millionaires.

So much was changing for me, and it all began the day I sat down in a hypnotist's chair and he told me I was good enough, important, and special, and could do anything I set my mind to. In the short time since Don had died, I was a traveling speaker and best-selling author—amazing! I was moving slowly and steadily through the grieving process and learning how to live as a single woman.

———— ∽∽∽ ————

I want you to be as successful as I was, but the good news is you don't have to spend $400K. Let me save you a significant amount of money so you don't have to go hire a bunch of mentors to reap the benefit of their teachings. I'm sharing all the goods with you in this book.

Let's do a quick recap of what you've learned. Every day our limiting beliefs and fears hold us back from reaching our fullest potential. This program has walked you through learning how to let go of your limiting beliefs that keep you stuck. You're building the foundation of your house so you can exercise a lifetime of tools to keep you on the path to lasting happiness. You're becoming an unstoppable manifesting machine because you know how to reprogram your mind.

Think about the assessments you did when you began this journey: the Wheel of Life and Stress Symptoms Checklist. In a minute you'll be retaking those assessments to see the progress you've made.

Over the course of this book you've been learning the importance of reprogramming your subconscious mind. We discussed identifying your kingpin belief and removing the logjam it created in your mind that kept you from fulfilling your goals. You don't have to take each log and haul it out of the way. Loggers will tell you, you just need to find the one log that is holding the logjam in place. Find the one and remove it, and the water will start to flow again. Find the root cause of your core belief that created this kingpin, and chop it down.

The powerful manifestation formula, Beliefs + Thoughts + Feelings + Actions = Results, taught you that your beliefs lead to your thoughts, your thoughts lead to your feelings, your feelings lead to your actions, and your actions lead to your results. So, if you aren't getting the results you want, back up to the previous element on the equation.

Our own limiting beliefs of what we're capable of hold us back from taking the actions we need to get the results we want. What's holding you back from losing those extra pounds, taking care of that money situation, fixing that relationship, and ending the dependence you have with cigarettes, once and for all?

You also learned about the discovery of the decade: neuroplasticity. Research has proved that you are a programmable biocomputer, but you need to reprogram your software so it isn't running on your stinkin' thinkin'. Your subconscious beliefs are not hardwired. You can install new beliefs and change the way your brain processes your thoughts. New thoughts and behaviors create new neuropathways.

We also talked about the power of "I am" statements and positive affirmations. I told you about the Willingness Mantra and the way the universe sends you what you're thinking.

> *The universe will send you what you are thinking about!*

Now you are ready for the fifth and final step to get you the results you want.

REASSESS

We'll begin by retaking your Wheel of Life and Stress Test Symptom assessments. Go back to your initial Wheel of Life, and using a pen of a different color, go through the assessment, circling the number that reflects where you believe you are in each category. We are looking for improvement, but change takes time, so keep your expectations in line with the short amount of time you've spent reading this book. You saw the before and after picture of Krista's and Kelsey's Wheels of Life. Expect results!

The goal is to be in balance—instead of a flat or wobbly tire, we see a smoother wheel. To be considered fully balanced, you're looking to have answers in the 8–10 range. If you circle a number less than 8, this is an area where you have blocks and limiting beliefs. Later in the chapter I'll share some specific affirmations and hypnosis sessions that can help you continue to improve in specific areas that aren't yet scoring 8 or higher.

HABITS

One of the most important components of finding lasting happiness involves everyday habits. I've talked to you about habits in various parts of this book, but I can't overestimate the power habits have on whether we succeed in this life.

I want to share a poem I read in Napoleon Hill's book *Think and Grow Rich*.[1] Versions of this have been circulated and modified by many others. It is sometimes referred to under the title "Your Servant" or "I Am Your Constant Companion." Can you guess who or what the poem is talking about?

I am your constant companion.

I am your greatest helper or heaviest burden.

I will push you onward or drag you down to failure.

I am completely at your command.

Half the things you do might just as well be turned over

to me and I will be able to do them quickly and correctly.

I am easily managed—you must merely be firm with me.

Show me exactly how you want something done and after a few

lessons I will do it automatically.

*I am the servant of all great people and,
alas, of all failure, as well.*

Those who are great, I have made great.

Those who are failures, I have made failures.

I am not a machine, though I work with all the precision of a

machine plus the intelligence of a person. You may run me for

profit or run me for ruin—it makes no difference to me.

Take me, train me, be firm with me, and I will place the world at

your feet. Be easy with me and I will destroy you.

Who am I?

I am Habit!

UNDERSTANDING THE MEANING BEHIND THE WORDS

I want to break down this poem into sections so we can unpack the wisdom this author is sharing and so you will have a greater understanding of how habits can either help you or hurt you.

"I am your greatest helper or heaviest burden."

Your subconscious mind seeks to meet your deepest needs, desires, and expectations. And your imagination is always more powerful than reality. Your SM doesn't know the difference between your imagination and reality. It is simply your servant. It listens to your conscious thoughts and does everything within its power to make your thoughts come true. It really is like a self-fulfilling prophecy. So, what are you telling yourself?

As I've said before, start listening to that inner voice that beats you up all day long and learn to train it to be your best friend, not your enemy. If you can make it your biggest cheerleader, you'll see so much progress.

"I will push you onward or drag you down to failure. I am completely at your command."

Whoa! That line sounds fairly ominous, doesn't it?

For example, the first time a person smokes a cigarette, it is not a habit. On day five it is not a habit. On day twenty it is not a habit. They could put down the package and walk away. But if they keep smoking for twenty-one to twenty-eight days in a row, it then becomes a habit, and the subconscious mind will resist when you try to quit. It takes, on average, about twenty-one to twenty-eight days to form new habits or break old habits (both good/bad) in your subconscious mind.

The same thing happens when you eat that first chocolate bar or bag of chips. It's not a habit unless you keep eating a single bag daily for twenty-one to twenty-eight days. Then your body is going to crave the sweet and salt of those fat-laden treats.

"Half the things you do might just as well be turned over to me and I will be able to do them quickly and correctly. I am easily managed—you must merely be firm with me. Show me exactly how you want something done and after a few lessons I will do it automatically."

Habits get formed by consciously thinking about the step-by-step actions required to get what you're craving. In other words, you literally learn how to adopt a new habit piece by piece.

Think back in time to the first time you tried to brush your teeth. You did not know that you had to hold the toothbrush a certain way in your hand or that you had to put toothpaste on the toothbrush. You did not know that you had to move the toothbrush back and forth, and up and down, across your teeth, and you did not know that you had to take a sip of water, rinse your mouth out, and spit.

Every day for a period of twenty-one to twenty-eight days you did the same thing over and over again, until the how-to part slipped into your subconscious mind. Suddenly you didn't have to think about how to brush your teeth—you just did it. Now it's a permanent habit in your subconscious mind.

How about the first time you drove a car? You did not know where to put your feet, what the different pedals were used for, where the signal lights were located, or when to use the emergency brake. Someone had to teach you, step-by-step, day after day, exactly what to do. Today, you do not have to think about it because you've formed a permanent habit in your subconscious mind. Basically, everything you do throughout your day is a learned habit that was formed from the moment you took your first breath after being born.

"I am the servant of all great people and, alas, of all failure, as well. Those who are great, I have made great. Those who are failures, I have made failures."

In reality, you learn how to dehypnotize yourself from negative/failure thoughts and replace them with affirmative/positive thoughts by learning to use self-hypnosis. Research has proved that just listening to a positive affirmation recording (at home or in your car on the way to work) ten minutes a day repeatedly can change negative programming that you have had for years.

For example, you have the power to change your bad habits by repeating some of the positive statements in the next sentence to yourself for twenty-eight days in a row.

I am slim and trim.

I am a nonsmoker.

I am in control.

I am happy.

I am successful.

I am calm and relaxed.

Nothing tastes as good as slim and trim feels.

Changing your habits really is a *"Fake it until you make it!"* lesson. By learning how to use self-hypnosis on your own to form new, healthy habits in your subconscious mind and quit self-sabotaging yourself, achieving your goals gets much easier.

If you hear that little inner critic, that little Tasmanian Devil, sitting on your shoulder, knock him off and tell him to go bother someone else. You are not going to listen to him anymore. You are not going to allow negative thoughts to enter your mind, and you won't tolerate any interference from him from this moment on.

"I am not a machine, though I work with all the precision of a machine plus the intelligence of a person. You may run me for profit or run me for ruin—it makes no difference to me. Take me, train me, be firm with me, and I will place the world at your feet. Be easy with me and I will destroy you. Who am I? I am Habit!"

According to research done by Stanford University and recorded by Patrick Porter on his CD *Theater of the Mind*, one of the theories about hypnosis and the mind states that it would take eighteen months for you to make a change personally if you did everything right. Imagine! Eighteen months of having to live fully on a conscious level, going around doing everything right. That means one day at a time, for eighteen months, doing everything right! Without emotion, without anger, without negative thinking—period.

However, what their testing proved was amazing. Through self-hypnosis and the use of creative visualization, you could make a mind change within just twenty-one days.

What does that mean for you? If you set the stage in your mind to create the change you desire and you rehearse it, you can literally take months off your learning process and become who you want to be quickly—in as little as twenty-one days.

That is why self-hypnosis is the quickest and easiest way to change your bad habits. All your good and bad habits are stored in your subconscious mind, and that's the part directly affected through self-hypnosis.

Here's an example of the work I did with one of my clients. She came to me and said she wants to break a specific habit of craving sugar and sodas. I gently guided her into a relaxed state of self-hypnosis by having her listen to one of my self-hypnosis sessions. As she relaxed, her conscious mind, the inner critic, got bored and distracted. At this point she was in the most highly suggestible state for her subconscious mind to accept positive reinforcements in her behavior, which would help her achieve her weight-loss goals.

I then gave her the idea that sugar and sodas no longer had the same seductive appeal to her they once had. They are not good, nor are they bad. They are just not important anymore. From that moment on she lost her desire for sugar and sodas. She then reinforced the suggestions I gave her by listening to self-hypnosis and positive affirmation CDs daily for twenty-eight days, until she had formed a permanent habit in her subconscious mind.

She no longer had those irresistible cravings she once had for sugar and sodas.

Just imagine being able to reprogram your thoughts so you no longer craved sugar. How about if you no longer desired to smoke, overeat, or do any other negative behavior you've been carrying around with you for so long? What bad habit are you ready to break starting now?

THREE EASY WAYS TO KICK YOUR BAD HABITS TO THE CURB

I could have written down at least a dozen ways to help you get rid of your bad habits, but I didn't want to overwhelm you with too much information at one time. We've talked about the impact using positive affirmations has, the reinforcing strength behind the Willingness Mantra, and the power of self-hypnosis. But let's get specific.

If you are ready to kick those bad habits to the curb for good, here are my top three winning solutions:

1. Work privately with a certified hypnotist to jump-start kicking your bad habits. Be sure to ask your hypnotist where they received their accreditation, as some are definitely better than others.

2. If your bad habit pertains to being overweight or eating unhealthy food, I invite you to check out my Ultimate Weight Loss Solutions Combo Pack or my *Weight Off NOW! Get Healthy—Get Happy Self-Hypnosis Home Study System*™. I share step-by-step methods on what you can do to overcome your

barriers to success, achieve the results you desire, and get on your way to living the life you've always wanted!

3. Utilize the power of a variety of self-hypnosis and positive affirmation MP3s. If you're interested in my recordings of positive affirmation and hypnosis downloads to listen to, check out my website and click on "Products."

"Products" page of Linda's website

Here's a rundown of the sessions you may find address the specific area where you're weakest (Remember this list?):

- Would you like to be happier? Use Positive Affirmation "Achieve Success."

- Would you like to love yourself more? Use Positive Affirmation "Self-Confidence."

- Would you like to eliminate negative thinking? Use Positive Affirmation "Self-Confidence."

- Would you like to learn to eat healthier? Use Positive Affirmation "Healthy Living."

- Would you like to improve your sleep? Use Positive Affirmation "Improve Sleep."

- Would you like to have more self-confidence and self-esteem? Use Positive Affirmation "Self-Confidence."

- Would you like to reduce stress? Use "Ultimate Relaxation" and "Reduce Anxiety" positive affirmations.

- Would you like to reduce pain? Use Positive Affirmation "Release Pain."

- Would you like to eliminate headaches? Use Positive Affirmation "Eliminate Headaches."

- Would you like to improve your memory? Use Positive Affirmation "Improve Memory."

- Would you like to train your inner critic to be your best friend? Remember to knock him off your shoulders and tell him to go get lost.

- Would you like to lose weight? If you only need to lose up to fifteen pounds, use "Ultimate Weight Loss Solutions"; if you need to lose over forty, use my "Weight Off Now! (WON)" program.

- Would you like to stop smoking? Use the "Stop Smoking NOW!" Combo Pack.

- Would you like to live well? I recommend the "Wheel-of-Life" Bundle.

I have thousands of testimonies from clients who've shared how my program helped them sleep better, find their self-worth, lose weight, gain the confidence to go after their dream job, improve relationships, you name it. I want to share just a few:

> I want to share some of the positive experiences that have happened to me since I participated in Linda Allred's ACT™ (now MindSonix) VIP Mentorship program. I came to Linda wanting to improve three areas of my life, namely my relationship, financial, and health aspects. Even though I know what my true passion and desires are, for some reason I felt stuck whenever I made any forward movement toward my goal of becoming successful in my part-time health and wellness company, as well as my personal life. It seemed that whenever I wanted to pick up the phone or go up to a person and share my business/products with them, I would have this self-defeating feeling, and negative thoughts came up, which blocked me from moving forward. It was really maddening because I could identify it but couldn't conquer it.
>
> In my sessions with Linda, to my surprise and delight, we were able to pinpoint the exact set of limiting beliefs, my "kingpins," and change the energy that they held over me.

Once they were identified and deleted (changed), a peaceful-ness came over me, like I had always been that way.

Within the first day of my program with Linda, I attracted a customer that literally jumped off a chair to grab me, wanting to know all about my products, and he bought everything I suggested!

What an exhilarating experience. As a result of this type of energy, I was able to quickly climb up another level in my business effortlessly. As far as my relationship goes, let me just say that I feel as if I'm on a second honeymoon!

Bottom line? You owe it to yourself to invest in working with Linda to get rid of your limiting beliefs! Love you, Linda!

—MARION CHAUVIN,
INDEPENDENT AMBASSADOR FOR PLEXUS WORLDWIDE

Here's another one:

Success was taking its toll on everyone in my business, including me. A hundred deadlines to meet, not enough time, schedules in disarray, worry, work and frustration were wearing me down. Then one of my employees brought in a brochure about a new Reduce Stress NOW Self-Hypnosis Home Study System™ Linda Allred was offering. I sent one of my colleagues to see Linda, and she returned to the office totally in awe of what she'd experienced. That's when I made the decision to try hypnosis and working with Linda to get some relief from my problems with stress. After one hour the gnawing pressure was gone. I felt totally relaxed, calm, and revitalized. My mind stopped racing, and I felt whole again. I've become more effective in both my business and personal life as a result of hypnosis. I finally have balance and har-mony in my life again. In my opinion, working with Linda is a bargain. As a matter of fact, I get large returns on my investment daily, and I like having control of my life again. Thanks, Linda!

—BERT FIFE, BATON ROUGE, LOUISIANA

You are more likely to succeed in achieving your goals if you commit to listening daily to these sessions. You get out of it what you put into it. If all you do is read this book and put it on a shelf, you won't get the results you're hoping for.

My clients have found that listening to my positive affirmation and self-hypnosis recordings boosted their success rate by at least 90 percent. When listened to repeatedly, affirmations begin to replace old, negative thought patterns with new, more positive ones, which helps cement a healthier and more receptive mindset.

There is no doubt in my mind that making changes in your lifestyle can be tough, so use any methods that work for you to help incorporate a more healthy, winning weight-loss program into your life.

Use the power of your subconscious mind to start living your best life possible. Learning the power of your thoughts and mastering them to achieve your greatest potential is a lifetime tool that no one can ever take away from you.

MINDSONIX

For those of you interested in taking a deeper dive into the mind, my mentor Nikkea B. Devida offers a process we've referenced many times in this book, MindSonix. MindSonix is a robust process that uses kinesiology, or muscle testing, to directly communicate with the power of your subconscious mind and guide you through the five-step C.L.E.A.R.™ process to reprogram your limiting subconscious beliefs.

Nikkea B. Devida offers this subconscious belief-change process, and because you have stuck it out to the end of the book, I know you are more than just dipping your toe in the water. As a gift, Nikkea has graciously agreed to offer you 50 percent off the cost of her program. All you have to say when you connect with her is, "Linda gave me a 50 percent off Happiness Coupon," and she will honor it.

I can tell you from personal experience that Nikkea's work is powerful and helps people go deeper into why they may score weakly in certain categories. Her system will teach you how to identify and change your kingpin belief in your subconscious mind so the logjam can get cleared.

Nikkea's email

www.MindSonix.com

EAGLES AND CHICKENS, A STORY WITH TWO ENDINGS

You may have heard this story before about eagles and chickens. I first read this story from the book *Hypnotherapy for Body, Mind, and Spirit* by Dr. Paul G. Durbin. I've changed it around a bit, but the takeaway message is the same.

A woman found an eagle's egg and put it in a nest of a fat barnyard hen. The eagle hatched with the brood of fat chicks and grew up alongside them.

All her life, the eagle watched what the fat barnyard chickens did, thinking she, too, was a fat barnyard chicken. She scratched the earth for worms and insects and watched the other plump barnyard chickens constantly overeat all day long. She watched the fat barnyard chickens lay around all day long and not exercise. She would thrash her slender wings and fly a few feet into the air and fall.

Years passed and the eagle grew to adulthood. One day she saw a magnificent slender bird high above her in a cloudless sky. It glided in graceful majesty among the powerful wind currents with scarcely a beat of its strong golden wings.

First ending

The eagle looked up in awe and said, "What's that?" Her fat barnyard chicken friend answered, "That's the slim and trim eagle, the queen of birds. She belongs to the sky. We belong to the earth—we are just fat chickens."

So the eagle lived and died a fat chicken, for that's what she thought she was.

Second ending

The eagle looked up in awe and said, "What's that?" Her fat barnyard chicken friend answered, "That's the slim and trim eagle, the queen of birds. She belongs to the sky. We belong to the earth—we are just fat chickens."

The eagle went through the day thinking about the slender eagle flying high. The next day, the eagle went down to the pond and saw her reflection. She noticed that she was fairly slim and trim and looked a lot like the slender eagle.

She began to test her wings, flying farther and farther each day, getting more exercise and gaining strength and muscle. After a few weeks, she was flying high and gliding just as if she were a slender eagle.

Suddenly, she had a mind shift and truly *believed* that she was a slender eagle and not a fat chicken. With that thought she flew above her past and her environment and let the slim and trim eagle that had been trapped within her soar.

Just like this eagle, how your story ends is up to you!

Dear reader, I hope you feel encouraged and inspired to live a life of lasting happiness. As part of my commitment to your success, I'd like to gift you with my Stress-Free NOW Self-Hypnosis Home Study System, which retails for $97.

All I ask is that you share your experience with someone else whom you think could benefit from what you learned in this book.

Stress-Free NOW! Self-Hypnosis Home Study System is a comprehensive digital program

Stress-Free NOW! Self-Hypnosis Home Study System

designed to help individuals overcome stress, reduce anxiety, and achieve ultimate relaxation through the power of self-hypnosis. Here's what the Home Study System includes:

- Stress Free NOW Overview—A comprehensive overview of the Stress-Free NOW program, outlining its objectives and benefits for users.

- 4-Part Video of the Ultimate Weight Loss Solutions Seminar—Gain access to a series of four informative and empowering video sessions from the Ultimate Weight Loss Solutions Seminar, providing additional value beyond stress reduction.

- Educational Materials—Supplementary educational materials to complement the video seminar sessions, offering valuable insights and guidance on stress management.

- Positive Affirmation MP3—Reduce Anxieties—An affirming audio session aimed at reducing anxiety and promoting a sense of calm and tranquility.

- Positive Affirmation MP3—Healthy Living—An affirming audio session designed to support individuals in their journey toward a healthier lifestyle.

- Self-Hypnosis—Ultimate Relaxation—A self-hypnosis audio session focused on inducing deep relaxation and alleviating stress, providing users with a soothing experience.

- Bonus: Self-Hypnosis—I Am Slim & Trim—A bonus self-hypnosis audio session aimed at promoting weight loss and fostering a positive body image, providing additional value to users.

HE WON THE RACE!

Do you remember little Dino from step 2? After his teacher called to ask what his parents were doing differently, Dino's father called me and said, "I want you to keep working with my child. I know he's ten, but I want to gift him your Slim, Prosperous, Perfect program. I don't care what it costs. This is my gift to my child."

So Dino came into my VIP, Slim, Prosperous, and Perfect program. I continued working with him with positive affirmations and listening to hypnosis sessions. I wondered about using MindSonix with Dino, so I talked with Nikkea, and she told me kids respond really great, so the next time Dino came in the office, I said, "We're going to play a game, Dino. Miss Linda has a magic wand. What if you could change your life and lead a brand-new life seven days a week, twenty-four hours a day? What would that life look like, Dino? Miss Linda's got her magic wand."

He said, "Well, Miss Linda, I need more self-confidence. And I need to make better grades."

"OK, we can put that in an overall goal because what we want to do is present a goal to your subconscious mind that this is the life I want to live and then find out all the kingpins holding you back." Then I asked him, "What else do you want? Is there anything else?"

I could hardly hear him, but he said, "Miss Linda, they tell me I'm really good in gymnastics. But every time I screw up, I just quit and go sit on the bench and pout."

I asked him why.

"I don't think I'm good enough."

Kingpin...Kingpin...Kingpin.

So we put all these into an overall goal for him. I then tapped into his energy, using muscle testing, and presented it to his subconscious. I found all the kingpins. Soon after, he successfully completed the program.

About two months later his dad called me. "I have something to tell you." He explained that Dino had tried out for a state gymnastics meet in his age group. "But Linda, when Dino got to the pommel horse, he stumbled."

My heart just sank. Dino...

Then Albert continued. "But the kid picked himself up, and you'll never believe it. He still won the meet!"

Every time I tell that story, I get goose bumps. I was so excited for Dino. Do you know why he won that race?

Because he believed in the deepest part of his subconscious mind that he could do it. And so he did it. I want your story to be like Dino's—a story of you overcoming all your bad habits, your negative thinking, your fears...Yours is a story of transformation and success.

You make a difference in the world by doing something that reflects your authentic purpose. By purchasing this book, you've proved your commitment to letting the world know that you are *tired* of feeling sick and tired, and you are ready to stand up and make a change. And I know you will do what you need to do to make it happen. No way would you have read this much and then decide to just put the book on the shelf and forget about it.

Just a few final thoughts as I reflect on our work together through these five steps: Remember, when you first looked into the mirror, you saw this little, tiny kitty cat, but now you're looking like a lion, moving into greatness, because you now know how to reprogram your mind. You are willing to do today what most people won't because tomorrow, tomorrow, you will have what most people won't.

STEP 5 CHAPTER TOOLBOX

What is the biggest takeaway from this chapter? Why?

_____

_____

_____

_____

What am I going to do today to be successful in achieving my goal? Then look at what you wrote in your "Roadmap to Success" and put it to use in achieving your goals.

_____

_____

_____

_____

Now that you've completed all five steps, what's your next move? Are you committed to beginning your transformation?

_____

_____

_____

_____

_____

MY ROADMAP TO SUCCESS

What am I going to do today to be successful in achieving my goal?

1.

_____

_____

_____

2.

_____

_____

_____

3.

_____

_____

_____

4.

_____

_____

_____

5.

_____

_____

_____

6.

_____

_____

_____

7.

_____

_____

_____

8.

_____

_____

_____

9.

_____

_____

_____

10.

_____

_____

_____

MY HAPPY ENDING

THROUGH ALL THE difficulties in my life, I've learned that life goes on, and we all have to make a choice. We can choose to be happy or choose to be sad by what we allow our minds to think about. I choose to be happy. I had a few more trials, though, to overcome before my happy ending.

FLOODED

After his death, I remained in the house Don and I lived in. I still operated my business out of my home. In 2016 Louisiana was hit by a slow-moving storm that dumped twenty inches of rain over three days. Thousands of homes flooded in an area categorized as a five-hundred-year flood zone.

According to *The Advocate*, "East Baton Rouge, Ascension, Livingston and Tangipahoa parishes saw the most widespread flooding. In all, it's estimated that 50,000 to 75,000 structures flooded, according to the National Weather Service, and 13 people died in the flood."[1]

I created a GoFundMe page and shared the following story:

> My name is Linda Allred. I am a widow of 3+ years and operate my business out of my home in Baton Rouge, LA. I am a best-selling author, certified hypnotist expert, and the founder of The Hottest Ticket in Town and Cracking the Weight Loss Code.
>
> The purpose of this GoFundMe request is to help me get

my business back up and running. I have nothing…not even a pencil. I really need 2 of most everything—desk, chair, paper, printer, computer, etc., so my office manager and I can get back to work. My plans are to move back into my home by Christmas, hopefully.

I love my job and I love helping people and I would be forever grateful for any amount you are able to donate.

The flood that hit my community of Baton Rouge on August 14th has literally taken me, as well as the people in the 20 surrounding parishes, to our knees as the muddy brown water flooded our communities and claimed all of our worldly possessions.

I personally received five feet of water into my beautiful 47-year-old home, as did my vehicle. Everything I own is sitting in front of my home in a pile of wet, broken, stinking, smelling trash. All that is left in my home is three commodes and studs, as the sheetrock and flooring have been removed to avoid mold.

On Sunday, August 14—the morning of the flood—I woke up at 3:17 a.m. when my generator kicked on. I smiled to myself, realizing I would have electricity. I never go to the bathroom in the middle of the night but thought "Hey, I will get up and sleep late." When my feet touched the floor and I felt water, my heart stopped. Minutes later, my neighbors Colleen and Steve called to say we were surrounded by water and the water was too deep to escape by car.

I let them know I had electricity and asked them to come over. They said they would as soon as they put some of their furniture up higher. I ran around like a crazy person packing my backpack, seeing the water get deeper and deeper by the minute.

I immediately called Mary, my office manager, who lives a mile away, and told her to wake up, that we were flooding. (She told me days later that I had saved her life, as well as Lola, her cat.) I then called my son Brian, who lives in Gonzales, about 35 minutes away. He said he was coming to get me, and to keep my cell phone charged. I said, "Brian, you will never make it."

Shortly after hanging up, another disastrous event occurred. All of the AT&T cell towers went down. I realized this when I tried over fifty times to call 9-1-1 only to realize the call would not go through.

An hour later, the water in my home had risen to three feet. I thought about trying to get the ladder at the back of the carport and climbing up on the roof, but when I opened the back door, a river of brown nasty water came rushing in. It was all I could do to shut the door.

"Linda, you are going to die," I whispered to myself. I made peace with God as I realized that I was either going to drown or be electrocuted from walking around in the water with the generator running.

This is when I decided to put a chair on top of my kitchen island and used a small ladder to climb up. There I was, sitting in that chair, when I heard knocking on my front window. I climbed down, wading into water now 4½ feet deep, to see my neighbor Steve at the window, telling me to raise the window and bust the screen out. The water was too strong and I couldn't get the screen out.

I rushed to the front door, but the water had already warped the door and I couldn't open it. Steve told me to try the living room window, and thankfully, I was able to remove that screen.

"Wait, Steve, I need to get my backpack," but Steve said the current was too strong, that I would never make it.

"We need to leave *now!*" What an angel Steve was, as he literally pulled me out of the window and into his arms. His son Matthew was helping his wife, Colleen. We were about a house away when I realized that I had left my cell phone, but Steve said we could not go back. "But Brian won't know what happened to me."

What happened next was nothing short of a miracle. We'd walked past two houses, struggling to stay upright in the wild, raging river of water when I saw a man coming toward us. The man said, "Mom, is that you?" And there was my son and grandson, Bryce. I immediately burst into tears as we all hugged. It was all we could do to get to safety where

Brian had parked his truck. We even stopped to rescue an elderly couple from the home Brian had parked in front of.

Brian and his family have taken me into their home, and I am so grateful as I am more fortunate that those who were forced to live on a cot in shelters throughout the city. Slowly, day by day, we are all trying to put the pieces of our lives back together, but I have to say, as much as I know about how to use my mind and keep myself positive, this disaster is a really humbling experience, one that literally takes you to your knees. I feel violated and traumatized.

I found out later that Mary had flooded out in her van trying to escape her flooded home, and the National Guard had to rescue her and take her to a shelter.

Every day, I force myself to be grateful for what I have instead of what I don't have because I understand that my subconscious mind (that makes up 95 percent of my mind) is listening to what I am thinking and is doing everything within its power to make my conscious thoughts true. I repeat over and over again, to myself, "All is well in my world because I know that I am held in the hands of God and I am perfectly, utterly safe, and so I am, and so I am."

One thing that has really helped me is listening to my Stress Free NOW! Combo Pack on my old laptop computer that thankfully did not flood (another miracle as it was sitting on top of a wicker bookcase that did not float and turn over). I would like to gift this combo pack to you. It has two Positive Affirmation MP3s: Reduce Anxieties and Healthy Living. It also has a beautiful self-hypnosis MP3: Ultimate Relaxation, designed to help you reduce stress.

All you have to do is contact me through my GoFundMe account and tell me you would like to receive it, and I will email you the download link as my "gift of gratitude." I know it will help you cope during these and other trying times. Also, if you need to talk, email me with your phone number and I will be happy to return your call and do everything within my power to help you.

My belongings on the side of the road after the flood

AFTER THE FLOOD

After my son and grandson rescued me from my flooded home, I lived with them for four-plus months. My granddaughter and grandson both wanted me to move into their bedroom, but I said no, and slept on a blow-up mattress. I cannot tell you how kind people were to me. They gave me clothes, money from the GoFundMe, shoes, and a purse.

I sold my flooded house for $150,000 less than it would have sold for the day before the flood and found a beautiful condo on the fourth floor (I was scared to live on the ground floor again) in a nice, safe area. The entire Baton Rouge community still to this day suffers from PSTD. But I smile now every time it rains because I know I will not flood way up this high.

My business, as well as all of Baton Rouge's business, hit rock bottom. My computer, all my hypnosis scripts and CDs, materials, clients' files, my entire business life was in five feet of wet, soaking mud. I remember crying myself to sleep one night and asking God, "What am I going to do?" When I woke up that morning, I had a great idea (it came from God, not me). I said, "Oh, I know what I can do."

Luckily, my laptop did not flood, as I had put it way up high the night before I flooded as a precaution, as all of Baton Rouge was flooding all around me. My laptop had all my recorded client sessions on CDs, all my products were on CDs—i.e., weight loss, stress, and stop smoking. So, I had all my CDs converted to MP3 digital files. That meant if someone wanted to work with me on Zoom, all I had to do was play the hypnosis session or send them my products with the MP3 link from DropBox. Wow! I was back in business.

Two or three months later I got a call from a gentleman who wanted me to customize a program for him teaching him my five steps. I remember taking a deep, deep breath and saying, "Your customized program, and your investment in yourself, is $8,000. What is the best credit card you would like to use, and I can see you either Monday or Wednesday next week. What would you prefer?"

He immediately gave me his credit card over the phone and paid in full, and we booked his first appointment. He loved the program so much that he enrolled his son in a customized program valued at $6,000. This was another God thing.

This money, and the $6,000 I had collected from GoFundMe, allowed me to pick up the pieces of my life again and restart my business. I would also like to mention that the International Women's Prosperity Network, out of Florida, that I am a member of also did a GoFundMe for me and gave me $2,500-plus. People are just so wonderful and kind.

You know, when my beautiful forty-seven-year-old house flooded, I did not have flood insurance because we never needed it. The day after I was rescued and moved in with Brian, I went down to the kitchen and saw Robin, my son's wife. She looked at me, and I said, "Robin, please hold me, I am not all right."

She held me in her arms and hugged me, and I sobbed in her arms, as I felt so violated. Everything I owned was flooded. I didn't even own a paper clip. My granddaughter had to give me a pair of her shoes because the raving floodwater tore them off my feet.

But day by day, life goes on, and God is good. Look at me now, living in this gorgeous, sassy condo in Perkins Rowe on the fourth floor.

My sassy condo

WORLD CRUISE AND STARTING OVER

The year 2020 was one of many firsts. I booked my first Holland America World Cruise, which began on January 4 out of Fort Lauderdale, Florida, and was scheduled to last four and a half months, ending on May 12. Two months into the cruise, on March 17, another first happened—at least in my lifetime: a worldwide pandemic. The cruise came to a halt.

I happened to be off the ship on a five-day excursion in the middle of the outback in Australia with eighteen shipmates when Australia blocked all ships from docking. Fortunately, Holland America flew us home, but it took the other 1,400 passengers two weeks to get off after negotiations with Australia. Our luggage took seven months to get back home to the US. Life is full of these very stressful times. Thankfully, I had a storehouse of tools to keep me calm.

Holland America generously offered us a makeup cruise since

we hadn't completed the one in 2020. So in 2023, as part of God's master plan, I boarded a ship, also leaving out of Fort Lauderdale, and was soon to encounter a person who would change the trajectory of the rest of my life.

After Don died, I had chosen to not pursue any other love relationships. The thought of having to take care of someone else again, of going through all the pain and suffering I went through as a wife and caregiver, would never happen to me again. I had a plan. If a man gave me that "interested" look, I would avert my eyes. And I'm happy to say my plan was successful—until I met Rod.

I must admit, my heart would melt when I saw older couples enjoying their time together. Most of us work our whole lives to finally have the time and money to go on fun trips. I remember going on one excursion in Casablanca, and an older man and woman were walking in front of me, holding hands. I gently tapped the woman's shoulder and said, "It's special to see the two of you holding hands." I asked them if I could take their picture.

At night I'd pray to God, telling Him I knew there was someone out there that I could love, but I was afraid to take that chance again and open up my heart. I asked God to find this man for me, but I needed the man to respect me and love me. It also would be nice if he were handsome and healthy, maybe interested in nutrition. I didn't want a man who was fat. Ideally, he'd have money to travel around and have fun. If he had a yacht, I wouldn't mind that.

I truly felt, even at the age of eighty-two, that I still had so much love to give someone. But I have to admit, the friends I hung around with were younger than me. The men I found myself attracted to were ten or fifteen years my junior. The problem was that the men my age looked like they had one foot in the grave already!

I would ask myself, "Linda, if you were a sixty-eight-year-old man, would you even look at someone my age, especially when you could probably attract a younger woman? I have been told that I do not look my age, and I really appreciate those comments. I tell people to hang around with me, and I will teach them how to live well.

My son Brian and his wife, Robin, came with me on the first leg of the world cruise, getting off the ship in Sydney, Australia. I continued on the next three legs of the cruise by myself. Two weeks later, in January of 2023, a lot of people onboard got sick with a cold that turned into bronchitis. Unfortunately, I was among them. I thought I would cough myself to death.

One day I went out on my veranda, and a man in the next cabin also happened to be out on his veranda. (I'll call him Peter, not his real name.) He leaned over and asked me how I was feeling.

"A little better," I said politely. Little did I know that Peter was single too, and he was out for a "score." He caught me in the hall a day or two later and asked me out. I told him no, still being polite.

"Well, maybe after the kids leave the ship," he suggested, having met Brian and Robin in the hallway earlier on the trip and learning they'd only be traveling with me for this first leg.

My son and his wife made a lot of friends on the cruise that were much younger than me, so I had the pleasure of hanging out with them. When Brian was about to disembark the ship in Sydney, he asked one of his friends, Trevan, for a favor. "When I leave the ship, will you keep an eye on my mom for me?" Trevan agreed.

Every now and then I would see Trevan, and he would ask me how I was doing. I told him Peter was still coming on strong. He said, "Linda, if he asks you out again, tell him you have a boyfriend, and you don't think your boyfriend would like you to go out with him."

Well, true to Peter's word, after the kids left, he caught me on the lido deck with a table full of his friends, and he asked me out again, upping his game this time by inviting me to the most expensive restaurant on the ship, The Pinnacle Grill.

Standing tall and with confidence, I proceeded to tell Peter I had a boyfriend and that my boyfriend would not approve of me going out with him. Of course, Peter wanted to know who my boyfriend was. I told him it was for me to know and for him to find out.

The next day, I saw Trevan and repeated my story. He said, "Linda, I will take care of this." I found out later he met with Peter and told him in no uncertain terms that I was not interested in him and to leave me alone. So that is how Trevan became my protector.

That night when I said my prayers, I informed God that He had completely gotten my request list for a man all wrong. Peter was not the one. If someone is going to steal my heart, I have to be number one and not just some lady on a long list of "scores."

～

I met Rod on February 5 in Greytown, New Zealand. I was on an excursion by myself, and we were at a restaurant for lunch. I looked around for a place to sit and saw a mother and daughter from the ship whom I knew, who were sitting with a man, and then one empty chair, and I asked if I could join them.

After we'd introduced ourselves, I took a look at Rod and thought, "He's cute." He had those "to die for" dimples, but when I looked into his eyes, he looked so sad and broken. I have never met a stranger, so we all had a lively conversation, and I do remember telling the group I was eighty-two years young.

Then the mystery of God's plan began to bring us together. I had booked all my excursions before boarding the ship on January 4, but I soon discovered that Rod had also booked many of the same excursions. When I would see him sitting by himself as I entered the bus taking us to where we were going, I would sit by him as a solo too.

The first time I sat next to him, he opened up about how his wife had passed away from cancer a year earlier. Rod knew how I felt. Here was a man that I could talk to who would understand what I had experienced, and vice versa, because if you have never experienced the pain and suffering of watching your spouse die before your eyes, you cannot imagine how painful this experience was. It takes you to your knees. I felt an instant bond with him.

I continued to meet Rod on excursions or at events on the ship, and we became friends. He and his wife had decided to sell his telecommunications company at the young age of fifty-seven so they could travel and see the world while she still had her health. Wow, this was a special man.

Rod was clearly still grieving the loss of his wife, and he certainly wasn't looking to date anyone new. In fact, he almost didn't go on the World Cruise that he and his wife had booked, but his family encouraged him to go, saying it might do some good instead of staying at home, looking at the same four walls he'd shared with their mom, his wife.

More weeks passed, and I wondered if Rod had any feelings other than friendship toward me, because I had feelings starting to develop. I had a plan that if he never said anything about it, I would casually ask him, "Do you want to share email addresses so we can keep in touch?" However, every time I would think to say this, the words would crawl right back down my throat.

"Linda, you are not going to chase this man. He is still grieving." By this point Don had been gone for ten years. I was in a different place on my grief journey. Rod didn't seem ready for a new relationship. So I waited for him to take the next step.

I wondered if Rod had heard me share my actual age when we first met. What if he didn't know and found out. Would that be a dealbreaker for him? I knew he was younger than me. But my attraction to him persisted. Earlier, on one of our excursions together, I told him I had a table in the dining room if he ever wanted to join our group of six for dinner. The one requirement I imposed was that only happy people could sit with me. Rod never showed up.

Later, he told me he could not sit at my table because he wasn't happy. One evening we were having a drink, and he said something that was the perfect segue for me to ask him his age. He told me that he was seventy years old. Then he asked me how old I was. I said, "I told you how old I was the first time we had lunch in Greytown."

"I don't remember," he said.

"I'm eighty-two years young."

He told me I certainly didn't look my age. Guess what! That night, he showed up at my table and met some of my friends. Amazing! The twelve-year age difference didn't seem to bother him.

The next night he found me dancing with some girlfriends in the ship's lounge, and he slipped onto the couch by me. As we were leaving, he said he would walk me to the elevator. While we strolled, he looked at me and said, "Don't you think it is time we go to dinner?"

"Yes, that sounds like fun."

Guess what day that was! May 8, five days before the end of the cruise. We'd been on the ship four and a half months, and he finally asked me out. Also, we could not get a reservation at The Pinnacle Grill until the night of May 10. I remember calling my sister when I got back to my cabin. "I just think this is a friendship dinner for helping him talk about his grief."

Walking into The Pinnacle Grill, I heard the maître d' whisper, "Sir Rod, I have seated you at a private table, per your request." I thought, "This doesn't sound like a friendship dinner." So, knowing me after half a glass of wine, I had the courage to say, "Rod, can I ask you a question?"

"Sure."

"Why did you ask me out?"

I fully expected him to say, "Because you have been so kind to me." Boy, was I surprised when he said, "Because I like you. You are real, and authentic, and I think you are beautiful."

Y'all, at that point, I almost slid under the table because it had been a long, long time since anyone ever told me that. Then he reached for my hand and leaned over and kissed me. I was over the moon.

And just guess who we ran into at the elevator after dinner, holding hands? Trevan. He stopped dead in his tracks and looked at me and said in a loud voice, "Linda, who is this man? I am your protector, and I don't know him." We all laughed, and I introduced Rod to Trevan but made him promise not to say a word to my son because I wanted to tell him in person.

Two days later we left the ship on the same bus, something

unplanned again, and then sat together at the airport, wondering when we would see each other again.

When Rod got home, he told his family he had met someone special on the cruise, and nineteen days later I picked Rod up at the New Orleans Airport, in a stretch limo, no less, and our new life, our new beginning, began. His grandson, Carter, said, "Papa, she must really like you if she picked you up in a limo."

Me picking up Rod from the airport in New Orleans in a limo

Later, I spent a month in Utah meeting Rod's family. Both of our families were happy we'd found each other. And now I am happy to say that Rod and I are retiring to the Great Smoky Mountains of Tennessee.

I truly believe this was all part of God's plan. The coincidences were just too many that we kept ending up at the same place over and over again with 1,600-plus people on this ship. Rod said he felt God talking to him too, saying, "Rod, pay attention; there is Linda again. Rod, pay attention; there is Linda again."

Now every night when I say my prayers, I always thank God for all my blessings and favors that He is sending my way. I always remind Him that He did really, really good when he put Rod in my life.

I smile as I go to sleep each night in Rod's arms, resting in the joy of finally finding someone who makes my life complete. And now I have someone I can hold hands with too!

"Out of your deepest wound in life calls forth your greatest gift to share." I came across this quote recently by coaching leader Jeffrey Van Dyk. In many ways his words sum up what I wanted to accomplish in writing this book. I've shared with you my journey to lasting happiness, and this book is now my gift to the universe.

Rod and me in Gatlinburg, Tennessee

RESOURCES

1. Hypnosis recordings:

    a. St. John's University (SJU) the book store. SJUnow.org

    b. LindaAllred.com under "Products."

2. Positive affirmations—I sell twelve on my website.

"Products" at
LindaAllred.com

3. Willingness Mantra—Sonia Miller's book: https://a.co/d/evYnO2k

4. Joyometer—Karin Volo's website: https://karinvolo.com
    Karin Volo is also the author of *1352 Days* as well as an e-book series titled *Bringing Joy to the World,* www.bringingjoytotheworld.com/joy-books.

MindSonix

5. MindSonix with Nikkea

6. *Rituals of Healing* by Jeanne Achterberg and Barbara Dossey: https://a.co/d/5fOcQQp

GO-TO GUIDE FOR SURVIVING THE IMPOSSIBLE USING POSITIVE AFFIRMATIONS AND SELF-HYPNOSIS

These were the tools I used during the hardest times in my life—my rocky relationship with Don, the grief of losing Wade, then Don, then to recover from the trauma of the flood, then when the world stopped at the onset of COVID and brought an end to my world cruise.

If you find yourself in unspeakable pain or trauma, make this your go-to list. If I can do this, so can you!

1. I lived in my Happiness Bubble. I refused to accept negative thoughts and tried to keep my mind positive. Did I succeed all the time? No. But a lot of the time.

2. I would scream positive affirmations out loud as often as I could: "Day by day, in every way, I am getting better and better than the day before!"

3. I listened to my MP3s.

   a. Positive Affirmations:

      i. Reduce Anxieties

      ii. Self-Confidence

      iii.Healthy Living

      iv. Improve Sleep

   b. Self-Hypnosis:

      i. Ultimate Relaxation

      ii. Greatest Secret

4. I used my Willingness Mantra

   a. Used my Joyometer

ACKNOWLEDGMENTS

MY HEARTFELT THANKS go out to the following:

Rod Hauer—the love of my life—for putting up with this crazy, creative lady who got up at all hours of the morning and stayed up late at night to write this story. Rod has been with me from the very beginning, when I first told him that I had a God Whisper and God wanted me to write a book so that I could help more people; then I could officially retire. I told him I felt as if I were birthing a baby and the baby was also ready to be born.

Nancy Matthew and Trish Carr of Women's Prosperity Network. They made this endeavor so much easier for me by offering their guidance and support.

Natalie Hanemann—my wonderful ghostwriter, who took my words (that were raw, and painful at times) and made them tender and meaningful.

Nikkea B. Devida—my mentor and friend who has been on this journey to lasting happiness with me from the very beginning, as we both want to spread the word (to the world) about how her system, MindSonix, can easily and quickly find the root cause of someone's problems and release it in a kind and gentle way so people can fulfill their dreams.

Lisa Sasevich—my mentor. Lisa, I want you to know what your mentorship did for me. You gave me the courage to be who Linda Allred needed to be. Not to hide in the shadows, but to be a bright light for those who will follow me. Writing this book has been both fun and painful, reliving how my husband treated me, calling me dumb and stupid, where I wanted to shrivel up and die, to throwing hot chocolate in his face one day, to learning to stand in my power and tell him how he treats me is totally unacceptable. Thanks from the bottom of my heart.

Loral Langemeier—my mentor. Loral, it was so much fun traveling throughout the US and Canada with you with your 3-Days to Cash team and getting to watch you behind the scenes, how you run your company. You taught me so many new skill sets, and I am forever grateful.

All my past mentors—Katrina Sawa, Chris Williams, Martha Hanlon, Russell Yarnell, Sonia Miller, Karin Volo, and all those whom I cannot remember.

My son, Brian, and Don's sister, Dee, who are OK with me telling my personal story of what went on behind closed doors as I struggled with sharing this part of my life. But I know that God wants me to share this story so that we can help more people learn to like, love, and respect themselves.

My sister, Janell, my best friend, who is always there for me and who is also struggling as a caregiver for her husband.

My duplicate bridge partner and friend, Belinda, another shoulder I could cry on and also share my happiness with.

Drs. Pam and Art Winkler and Chaplain Paul Durban, my hypnosis mentors. Without you I would not be who I am today.

And last but not least, all my clients who have supported me and referred clients to me.

ENDNOTES

PRELIMINARY WORK

1. These categories are based on Nikkea B. Devida's MindSonix™ program.

STEP 1

1. Katty Kay and Claire Shipman, "The Confidence Gap," *The Atlantic*, May 2014, https://www.theatlantic.com/magazine/archive/2014/05/the-confidence-gap/359815/.

2. Years ago, in my training with Nikkea B. Devida (ACT/Mindsonix), we were taught 1 percent and 99 percent, so that is what you will hear on the videos that accompany this book, but most sources cite 5 percent and 95 percent, respectively.

3. "Bruce Lipton Quotes," Elevate Society, accessed June 8, 2024, https://elevatesociety.com/quotes-by-bruce-lipton/.

4. "Understanding Unconscious Bias," NPR, July 15, 2020, https://www.npr.org/2020/07/14/891140598/understanding-unconscious-bias. In my previous printed material, I referenced another number, but that information is now outdated.

5. Dr. Caroline Leaf, *Switch on Your Brain: The Key to Peak Happiness, Thinking, and Health* (Grand Rapids, MI: Baker Books, 2013).

STEP 2

1. Dr. Deepak Chopra, a prominent author, speaker, and alternative medicine advocate.

2. "Marianne Williamson," Goodreads, accessed June 8, 2024, https://www.goodreads.com/quotes/3225323-ego-says-once-everything-falls-into-place-i-ll-feel-peace.

3. Marianne Williamson, *A Return to Love: Reflections on the Principles of a Course in Miracles* (San Francisco: HarperOne, 1996).

STEP 3

1. You can watch BBC coverage on Dr. Ewing discussing this story here: https://www.youtube.com/watch?v=u34HoFVxSNc.

2. "How Do Celebrities and Athletes Use Hypnosis?," Hemisphere Hypnotherapy, March 9, 2021, https://hemispherehypnotherapy.com/

celebrities-and-athletes-use-hypnosis/#:~:text=He%20claims%20it%20
helps%20him,and%20increase%20his%20mental%20stamina.

3. Luke 17:21, NKJV.

STEP 4

1. John 10:10, NKJV.

2. This magazine is no longer in circulation, and the stories were not archived. However, these statistics originally came from a hypnotist who did a presentation I attended at the Women's Prosperity Network years ago.

3. I put this list in the back of the book to be a quick go-to guide for dealing with times of extreme stress.

STEP 5

1. Napoleon Hill, *Think and Grow Rich* (Castle Books, 2015).

MY HAPPY ENDING

1. Advocate staff, "What caused the historic August 2016 flood, and what are the odds it could happen again?," The Advocate, August 5, 2017, https://www.theadvocate.com/louisiana_flood_2016/what-caused-the-historic-august-2016-flood-and-what-are-the-odds-it-could-happen/article_3b7578fc-77b0-11e7-9aab-f7c07d05efcb.html.

ABOUT LINDA ALLRED

Linda Allred, acclaimed as The Bad Habit/Belief Breaker, is a renowned figure in personal development. She is renowned for her expertise in assisting individuals and groups in overcoming the barriers preventing them from realizing their full potential.

With a rich tapestry of experience and knowledge, Linda is celebrated as a two-time best-selling author, captivating speaker, and transformative practitioner. Her debut work, *Answering the Call*, swiftly ascended to the coveted number one best-seller status on Amazon in two categories: Marketing and Marketing for Small Businesses. This compelling narrative chronicles Linda's journey from adversity to triumph, inspiring readers to liberate themselves from limiting beliefs and embrace their inherent greatness.

Her subsequent best seller, *Journey to the Stage*, unveils the secrets to commanding attention and unleashing the power of one's voice. *Journey to Lasting Happiness*, Linda's third book, is a masterpiece and transformative guide to living a healthy, prosperous, and joyful life.

Linda's contributions to personal development have earned her prestigious accolades, including a Quilly™ Award in Hollywood, California, in September 2014. Her impactful presentations have enthralled audiences alongside luminaries such as Mark Victor Hansen, Lisa Sasevich, and Peter Diamandis.

Armed with a Bachelor of Science degree in clinical hypnotherapy and currently completing her MA degree in counseling psychology at St. John's University of Southern California, Linda brings over three decades of passionate practice to her work by seamlessly integrating the latest advancements in science, spirituality, and psychology. Her holistic approach yields remarkable, enduring results for her clients. Certifications from the esteemed

National Guild of Hypnotists, and the International Medical and Dental Hypnotherapy Association further underpin Linda's expertise.

In 2010 Linda broadened her horizons by becoming a Certified Accelerated Change Template (ACT)™ Practitioner Expert, distinguishing her as one of the select few in the US certified in this transformative belief-change science. By integrating the energy work of applied kinesiology, known as muscle testing, Linda empowers individuals to effect profound mindset shifts, guiding them toward lives of happiness, health, and fulfillment.

Through her unwavering dedication and transformative methodologies, Linda Allred continues to empower individuals worldwide to unlock their inner greatness and live their best lives.

To arrange for Linda to speak at your company or event and to explore her books and programs, please contact her by email at linda@lindaallred.com, by phone at 225-275-2451, or on her website at LindaAllred.com.